The Best of...

The Joy of Tech

by **Nitrozac**
& Snaggy

O'REILLY®

Beijing · Cambridge · Farnham · Köln · Paris · Sebastopol · Taipei · Tokyo

The Best of the Joy of Tech
by Nitrozac and Snaggy

Printed in the United States of America.

Production Editor: Matt Hutchinson
Cover Designers: Nitrozac and Snaggy
Interior Designers: Snaggy and Ellie Volckhausen

Printing History:
November 2003:   First Edition.

Colophon:
The cover of this book was designed by Nitrozac and Snaggy and produced by Emma Colby with QuarkXPress 4.1 using ITC American Typewriter, CCSpills, and ITC Legacy Sans fonts. The interior layout was produced in Adobe InDesign 2.0. The illustrations that appear in the JoyPolls were produced using Macromedia FreeHand 9. Matt Hutchinson, Sue Willing, Melanie Wang, and Claire Cloutier provided quality control.

ISBN: 0-596-00578-4
[C]

Dedications:

For my dad, Rudolf Schmalcel, who loved jokes,
and believed "they're really going to make it."
I miss you Dad.

And for my mom, my rock in the stormy seas of life and
my lighthouse of love and support. I love you Mom!

Liza
(Nitrozac)

For Gord...gone now...but his laughter and love continue.

Bruce
(Snaggy)

Acknowledgments

Since its humble beginnings, The Joy of Tech comic has been published in many incarnations: on our web site, in magazines, newspapers, newsletters, on posters and T-shirts, coffee cups and boxer shorts, and by countless independent inkjet printers in cubicles across the Internet.

The interface you are holding now, *The Best of the Joy of Tech* book, is the first major print collection. Each comic has been selected by us, lovingly tweaked and digitally enhanced, pixels nitpicked and quips quibbled, and presented to you in glorious 300 dpi. Now, despite our addiction to all things binary, it is still quite a thrill for us to see our work on processed-tree product, and there are many people we wish to thank, without whom there would be no Joy in Geeksville.

First, we'd like to thank Tim O'Reilly and everyone at O'Reilly & Associates for their support behind this project, their patience, and their phenomenal commitment to printing this Joy in full color. Magnificent Valour!

Thanks to David Pogue, for his great sense of humor, and intellect, and talent, and for writing our Introduction, which incorporates all three of those qualities. David's enthusiasm and love of technology is as infectious as the Sobig worm; he's someone who really puts the *joy* in technology, and to have his bubbling effervescence here with us is, well, excuse us as we pee our pants in geek glee!!!

Steve Wozniak. Whoa. What can we say, except it's an honor and a privilege to share this time-stream continuum with you, and a whole lot of fun. Woz, your engineering skills have created so much joy for so many people, but it's your laughter that is the real apple of your eye. It is an inspiration.

To Ron Schmalcel and Dr. Harry Hoff, thank you so much for all that you have done and do. There would be no cartoon existence as we know it without your encouragement and partnership. And to Phyllis, without your unwavering love and support, and those Tim Horton drop-offs, we would have pulled the plug long ago.

Also much deserving of our kudos and gratitude is Dave DeMaagd (a.k.a. spinyNorm), who keeps "Fawn" turned on and who is *our* geek superhero. Sharon Akers, the CPU of Blackberry Hill—you rock! And endless indebtedness for the comic book customs that were passed down to us by Snaggy's brothers and by Mark.

To our sponsors and longtime supporters (like Jim at Roadtools.com) who keep our electrons flowing, thank you for helping bring Joy to our fans. And to everyone who has shopped at our webstore...thank you! There are a *lot* of propeller beanies spinning out there, and they've kept our comic explorations flying.

Infinite thanks to all the web sites that have spread the word about our work: places like MacSurfer.com, Powerpage.org, Macinstein.com, iPodlounge.com, Macmerc.com, and the countless blogs and homepages and forums across the global village. And we won't forget that Slashdot.org link a long time ago in a cartoon universe far far away. Thank you Rob and Jeff—a little HTML has gone a long way.

But most of all, thanks to our fans, whose page views and generosity have made JoT possible, and whose encouragement and friendship have kept the creative fires burning. To name just a few: DigitalBill, maswan, ilovemydualG4, GMx, Swiss Mercenary, chromatic, dragonman97, Super Flippy, Rednivek, Jessycat, supa, Steen, and LostInColorado. And thanks to all the Superfans, and to the many still lurking. :happytears:

Oh, and there's one more thanks...

Thank *you* for picking up this book! We do hope you enjoy the collection. We couldn't cram everything inside it that we had hoped to, but oh well, that's what Version 2.0s are for! Don't forget to do the bonus just-for-you online JoyPolls, and if you are new to joyoftech.com, please stop by the Forums and say hi.

enJoy!

Nitrozac and Snaggy

Early in life I had three strong directions: to be an engineer and a teacher (thanks, Dad) and to have a sense of humor (thanks, Mom).

Somewhere along the line, probably only a short while after Apple was started, I started speaking to interested groups. I never failed to communicate many stories of how we at Apple mixed fun and business, and even pranks. As we became successful I knew that it meant much less to me than the fun we had laughing at jokes and life. I had visions of two people on their deathbed, one who was successful, and another who had many more frowns than laughs.

So I came up with the formula $H = F^3$: Happiness = Food, Friends, and Fun. At a high school speech the students laughed and I realized there might be a 4th 'F.' The principal idea was that the measure of life was another formula: Smiles minus Frowns. It's easy to assign values to the people you know. Anyway, I have held true to this philosophy. My own friends tend to be the "interesting" people of this world, rather than the successful ones.

Engineers, especially when young or in school, particularly electrical technicians or software technicians, are placed in a unique position. Like chemists or physicists, they have knowledge of how to cause things to happen that others don't really understand. It's like an art of deception. A properly tuned transmitter might jam a TV set, and an ordinary person thinks that the TV is bad. When they adjust the TV controls (we actually had tuning and color dials in my youth), the picture improves. There's an element of comedy in the control this gives the geek.

Prolific computer users, software writers and hardware designers, the sorts that do these things all the time at home, generally wind up with dozens of stories of good pranks they pulled with technology.

The main element of creative design is thinking outside the box. In simple terms this means taking different approaches than those that are obvious but still achieving the desired result. The creative designer takes a new approach, which leads down a less obvious path but winds up being a shortcut.

This is much like humor. A typical joke deceptively leads your mind in one direction, and the punch line reveals that a second interpretation existed. This discontinuity makes us laugh and enjoy life. The elements that lead to product design are the same as those that make up jokes. If I had to live with one or the other, I'd choose the humor.

As engineers, what we are recognized for in our companies is creative thinking that converges on things that work. It is a labor of love because our salaries are but a fraction of the lawyers who work on company contracts, or of the people who sell what we design. Engineers tend to wind up in an us versus them situation where "them" includes marketing, business, lawyers, systems, procedures, beauracracies, and even unions (an engineer can't move a soldering iron from one bench to the next if a union guy is paid to do such things). So we make a lot of weak jokes about our environment and how they don't understand what we do, all day every day. When the jokes stop, it's time to move on I say.

The hardest time of my life was actually doing electrical designs or writing programs. I would keep dozens of related factors in my head and stare at code and try to think of ways to improve it. Intense concentration at the limits of what your mind can do is extremely stressful. It's not possible to work this intensely once you're older, like over 25.

So many of us become a bit strange to the rest of the world. It goes with the territory. We become the geeks who can have conversations with our own types that normal people just don't understand. Our lives involve unique aspects that bind us, like a religion without a church. Geek Culture is one of our primary places of worship. It not only makes us laugh, it gives our choice of occupation specialness and meaning.

It is great that this cartoon exists, to make us feel proud of who we are, while laughing a bit at the disconnects of real life. The Joy of Tech comic makes us all heroes. It makes me feel like I felt reading Tom Swift, Jr. books in elementary school — that engineers can save the world from all sorts of conflict and evil.

I have known Nitrozac and Snaggy (Liza and Bruce) for some time. They first visited me in 1999 and helped with my computer classes. These were talented people willing to share with eager 7th graders. Bruce and Liza created delightful fun projects for all the students. These are people with a heart. It mattered less that they look impressive to the youngsters than that the youngsters be filled with self-esteem. One project was to make buttons with photos that we took in class. From a project like that, the students came to realize that they had made something with a fairly normal computer and with applicable skill that few other students at school had. They truly felt special about these skills and others that Nitrozac and Snaggy brought to the class that day.

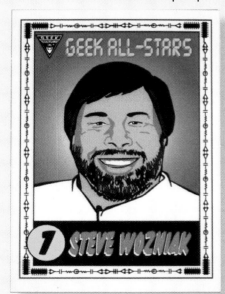

It's funny, but the things that are most important to me are people like Liza and Bruce and their strip, more than most of the projects I've ever designed or built.

Steve (is tv wake zone?)

Introduction by... The Fabulous DAVID POGUE

If *www.geekculture.com* is already one of your toolbar links in Internet Explorer, then this book needs no introduction whatsoever.

After all, you're already a fan of the one-of-a-kind comic strip for nerds known as The Joy of Tech. You already know that every other day or so, there's another delicious, full-color, vector-drawn comic. And you're plenty familiar with the central topic of The Joy of Tech: the interaction of humans and computers (and, with surprising frequency, of cats with computers).

To you, a description of the cast of virtual characters would be almost redundant: the overweight but lovable computer nerd and his hapless attempts to coexist with normal people, Bill Gates, Steve Jobs, the Dell Dude and other gigantic egos. Aliens. Pop culture.

And then there's that recurring freaky guy in the black suit and the bad comb-over. (I'll bet you $100 that with a little research into the cartoonists' childhood, you'd unearth a guy who looks exactly like that in some abusive authoritative position.)

Finally, of course, there are the babes. Quite frankly, Nitrozac and Snaggy draw the most luscious cartoon women since Jessica Rabbit. They fuel the fantasies of more lovelorn online geeks than the top 50 porn sites put together. (The babes, that is, not Nitrozac and Snaggy.)

Sometimes these curvy bombshells play realistic roles: as symbols of the unattainable, as teasing glimpses of a glamorous life that the true geek will never have, as the ultimate contrast to their own T-shirt-wearing, crumb-covered lifestyles. (Look for the one with the caption: "It was at that precise moment Stanley realized that he may very well be a brain in a vat.")

At other times, these beauties are geeks themselves. All right, *you* may not know many superfoxes who'd rather edit the Windows registry than—anything. But nobody ever said cartoons had to be realistic. ("Linux Lass"? Now *there's* a major motion picture not coming soon to a theater near you.)

In the end, though, you get the idea that the real stars of The Joy of Tech—the unkempt male schlumps who populate most of its panels—don't really mind not being Leonardo DiCaprio (or even the Dell Dude). They get their pleasure elsewhere: from RAM upgrades, from blogging, and from new, unattainably expensive PowerBook models.

Which brings up another point you, the JoT fan, know all too well: this is a cartoon that's not just drawn on Macs—more often than not, it's *about* Macs. You won't find a single strip that celebrates Windows (what could possibly be funny about such a tragedy of an OS, anyway?). That doesn't mean, though, that the Joy of Tech is all rah-rah pro-Macintosh. Lord knows there's a lot to laugh about in the land of Jobs, too, from Mac zealotry to the capricious decrees of His High Steveness. So, a warning: If you've never used a Mac, you might not get a few of the jokes. (Then again, as Nitrozac and Snaggy might tell you, that's not all you're not getting.)

Now, speaking of Nitrozac and Snaggy: those obviously aren't their real names. And to the shameless moochers who view the comic for free online, Nitrozac and Snaggy will have to remain mysterious code names forever.

But you, the discerning fan who went the extra mile to buy or borrow this book, are entitled to know just a little bit more.

Their real names are Bruce Evans (Snaggy, short for Snagalena, a character in a song he wrote about a cowboy who falls hopelessly in love with an alien) and Liza Schmalcel (Nitrozac, an inside joke that refers to "the ultimate anti-depressant"). He mainly writes, she writes and mainly draws (using a graphics tablet and Macromedia Fireworks).

They're Canadians. They met at art school, where they earned their artistic licenses in drawing and silicon-based art forms like electronics and holography. They're not technically married, but they behave as though they are. And they spend too much time away from civilization to know when they've gone too far. (Exhibit A: the time they posted, on their site, instructions for carving a jack-o-lantern into a likeness of Steve Wozniak. Exhibit B: the time they turned my head into downloadable Mac OS X folder icons. I didn't know whether to be flattered or hire a litigator.)

Yes, if you're a Joy of Tech fan, you knew all this. If you're unfamiliar with Nitrozac and Snaggy's oeuvre, however, you can get up to speed in either of two ways:

(1) Read this introduction from the beginning.
(2) Turn the page and enter the twisted, hilarious world of The Joy of Tech.

David Pogue

BOOT-UP!

```
--- ------ ------

I was going to boot up,
But then I got high.
I was really going to Start,
But then I thought "why?"
Now my registry's all messed up and I know why.
Because I got high,
Because I got high,
Because I got high,...
```

Your computer on drugs.

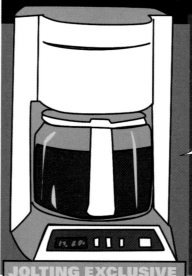

TROLLING
IN A NUTSHELL

by H4x0r
with an introduction by Anoynomous Coward

The perfect companion for the serious troll! This impressive, comprehensive guide to trolling now covers masquerading, faking accounts, beating the filters, ...all the "tricks of the trolls"!
Includes a handy offensive word reference!

A much 13370r book than Trolling for Dummies! btw.... First Post!

Protest march of Felines Against Flat Panel Monitors.

The Evolution of Patent Law.

Despite recent campaigns to raise awareness of the problem, anthropomorphization is still the leading cause of inter-species break-ups.

It was a mad, mad, mad, mad, really mad cow.

Geek Love

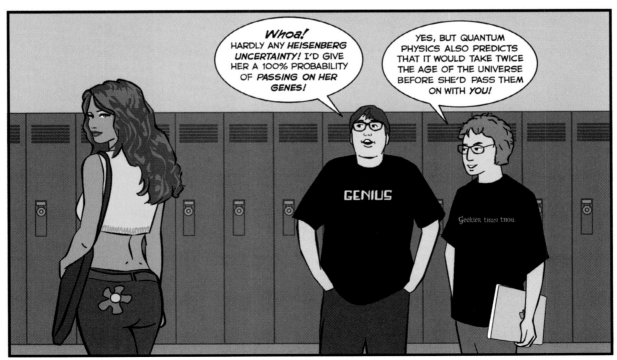

The quantum mechanics of girl-watching.

If you love some Geek...
set it free...
then watch it go online.

No one had informed him of *all the risks* of installing Linux.

How to Lose a Geek in 10 Seconds

- Surprise him by re-organizing all those icons on his computer's desktop for him!

- Throw out his current mousepad and replace it with one that has a picture of cute little kittens!

- Ask him to flex his mighty geek muscles for you by helping you sign up for an AOL account!

- Help him break his caffeine and junk food habit by hiding his coffee, cola, and chips!

- Prove to him that you are ready to *really commit* by asking him his root password.

- Announce that you've finally learned to program.... the VCR! It's a good thing too, as, all by yourself, you were able to record Oprah over those old Star Trek tapes!

- Stand behind him as he writes his email, helping him with his spelling and offering your suggestions.

- Motivate and inspire, by constantly reminding him to stop sitting at the computer and to do some work instead!

- Undoubtedly, he also loves Valentine's Day! Mention you can't wait to find out what he has planned!

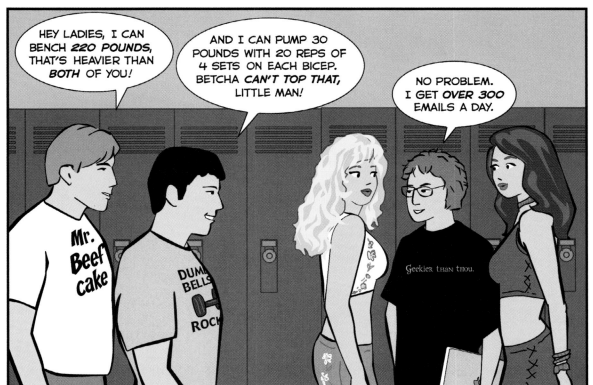

The new measure of strength.

Mrs. Greenfield, the wife of a third generation potato farmer, was shocked to discover her husband's corn site collection.

Sexual Dysfunction in Phallic Fruit.

Later that night, poor Sweetie would wonder why
his wife had him on "auto-headache".

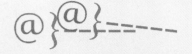

It was at that precise moment Stanley realized that he may very well be a brain in a vat.

HACKS AND CRACKS

GIVE ME YOUR LUNCH MONEY OR I'LL HACK INTO YOUR HOMEPAGE.

Millions of years of evolution are finally paying off for *Geeko Sapiens*.

They always dreamed of having a home *in* the range.

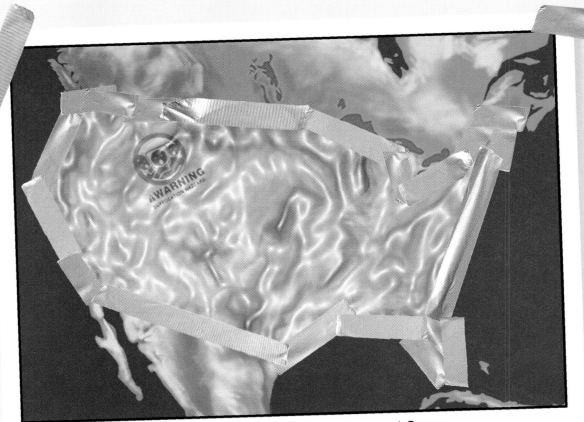
Homeland Insecurity: Duct Tape and Cover.

Genetic engineering using iPhoto2.

Little Bobby had made the mistake of using crypto without a government-approved backdoor.

It was perhaps not the smartest thing for Tim to burst out with during a Parasitology Convention.

It was at that precise moment Stanley realized that registering My-Boss-is-an-Idiot.com wasn't the smartest career move he had ever made.

He was luckier... the desk allowed him to work
in his underwear.

Luckily for Todd, his company had abolished
the once brutal practice of geek-breaking.

Techie-daze!

It was exactly what Luke and Leia were looking for... an "Evil Bastard" Father's Day Card.

THE LITTLE BRATS... I OUTTA THROTTLE THEIR *THROATS!*

It was that same age-old debate, as the two rival factions clashed over Easter weekend.

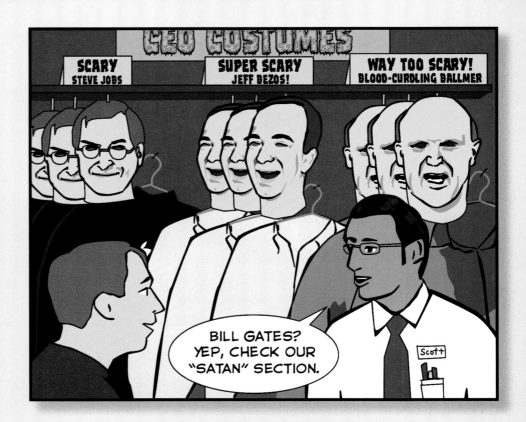

Klingon Turkeys.

Barbara Walters's first interview.

Another NORAD tradition... tracking Apple rumors on MacWorld Expo Eve.

NEW YEAR'S RESOLUTIONS

How about them *nix?

A few drinks and Tux's inhibitions were gone, resulting in a modeling session he would regret for the rest of his life.

On a related note, that was also the correct answer to
"Why Edward doesn't have a Girlfriend."

At Earth OS Fest, everyone enjoyed dressing up as their favorite GNU/Linux celebrity, except for Zap, who always seemed to get stuck playing Richard Stallman.

Hemos
(Lioness Baits)

Monopolus
Caesar

It was the Wild Wild Kernel,
and only one man could tame it!

Cmdr Taco
(Slashus Fanaticus)

"YEP, I INSTALLED THOSE PARTS MYSELF, NOT ONLY THAT, I HACKED THE KERNEL SPECIFICALLY FOR THE DRIVER! THIS BABY RUNS SMOOTH AS SILK, IT'S A SPEEDSTER TOO, I TELL YA!"

Last Will and Testament

I, being of sound mind and body, do hereby bequeeth to my grandchildren, my most cherished possession, something that took me years to acquire, and the one thing I cherish above all...

my Slashdot karma.

CowboyNeal
(Metus Moderado)

A Mac user's early triumph with Linux.

Penny always wondered if her son had inherited his father's Unix genes.

Another triumphant moment in Betty's brilliant Phonetics Investigator career.

If only it came in a non-abrasive formula.

LYNN NICKS, MILD-MANNERED LIBRARIAN, WHILE LOOKING FOR AN AROMATHERAPY WORKSHOP, ACCIDENTALLY STUMBLES INTO A LINUX USER GROUP MEETING!

UM, EXCUSE ME, IS THIS THE RIGHT ROOM?

THERE, THE COLLECTIVE HOPES AND DREAMS OF ALL THE USERS, CAUSE A WARP OPTIMIZATION RIFT, WHICH TRANSFORMS HER MIRACULOUSLY INTO...

LINUX LASS

SUPER LINUX EVANGELIST! SOFTWARE FREEDOM FIGHTER!

DEFENDER OF THE GNU AND THE OPEN SOURCE WAY!

WHILE WORKING AT THE LIBRARY, *LYNN NICK'S* SENSES BIG TROUBLE! SUDDENLY, *THE MAN* BURSTS INTO THE QUIET AREA!

LISTEN UP BOOK WORMS! I'M INSTALLING MY *PROPRIETARY OS* ON ALL LIBRARY COMPUTERS!

SNEAKING BETWEEN BOOK SHELVES, LYNN QUICKLY CHANGES INTO *LINUX LASS!*

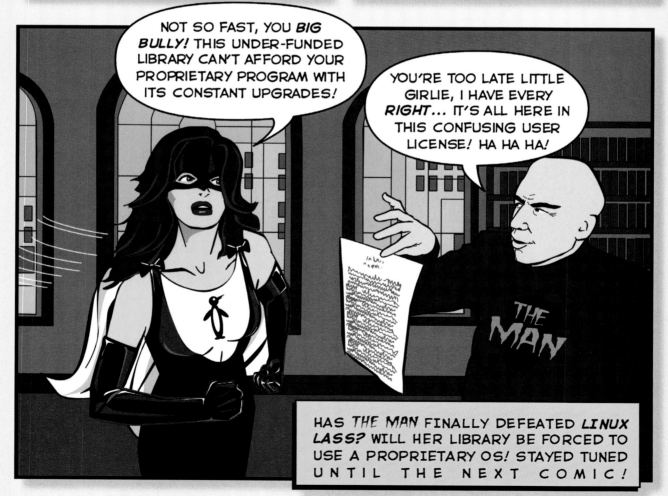

NOT SO FAST, YOU *BIG BULLY!* THIS UNDER-FUNDED LIBRARY CAN'T AFFORD YOUR PROPRIETARY PROGRAM WITH ITS CONSTANT UPGRADES!

YOU'RE TOO LATE LITTLE GIRLIE, I HAVE EVERY *RIGHT...* IT'S ALL HERE IN THIS CONFUSING USER LICENSE! HA HA HA!

HAS *THE MAN* FINALLY DEFEATED *LINUX LASS?* WILL HER LIBRARY BE FORCED TO USE A PROPRIETARY OS! STAYED TUNED U N T I L   T H E   N E X T   C O M I C !

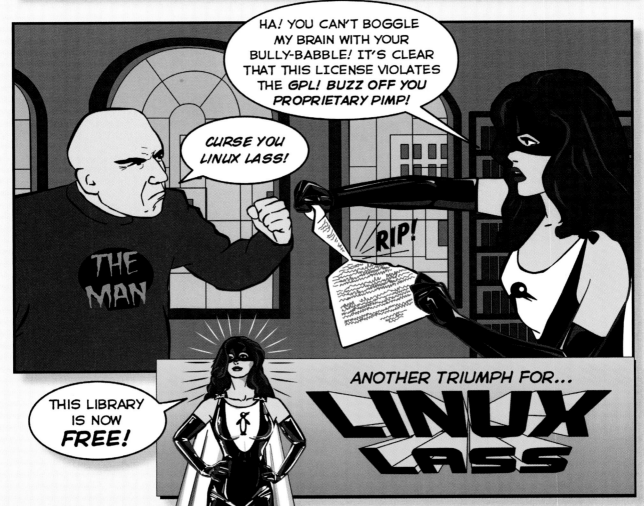

If only Steve's "one more thing" included this
hot little number *for the rest of us.*

HEY THERE ALL YOU *GEEKS* AND *GEEKETTES*... LET ME TELL YOU A SILICON TALE THAT'S BEEN PAST DOWN THE *GENERATIONS!* SO CURL ON UP BY THE HEATSINK AND *ENJOY...*

The Megahertz Myth

Once upon a time, in the mystical Land of Tech, there was a little chip named G4.

Now this chip was different. Unlike the other chips, he was smaller, and he had a lower megahertz. All of the other chips would tease poor G4, never letting him play the latest games, and laughing at him until he was at the point of short circuits.

One day, a Grand Expo was announced. All the chips were very excited to be invited to perform for the crowds. All except little G4, since he was told that he was too slow to go.

Poor little G4 was so sad...

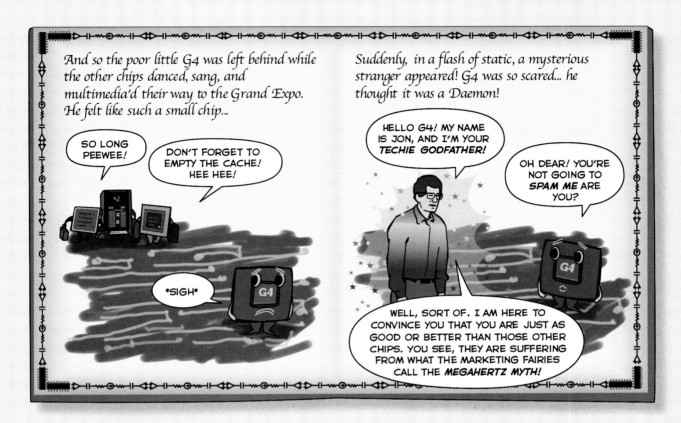

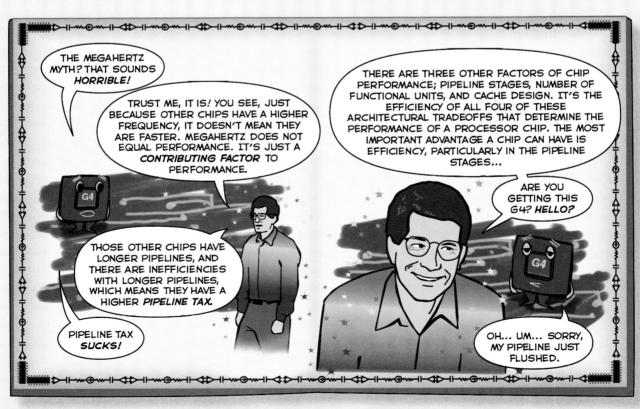

G4's Techie Godfather explains further...

PIPELINE STAGES IN CHIPS ARE LIKE A DIGESTIVE SYSTEM; FOOD IS *FETCHED* FROM THE MOUTH DOWN THE ESOPHAGUS TO THE STOMACH, WHERE IT'S *DECODED* BY DIGESTIVE FLUIDS, THEN NUTRIENTS *EXECUTED* FROM THE FOOD ARE *STORED*.

IMAGINE A *PIE EATING CONTEST* WITH TWO CONTESTANTS: AN ELEPHANT AND A MOUSE. BOTH SIT AT A TABLE, AND PIES ARE BROUGHT TO THEM TO BE "PROCESSED". AS THEY ARE EATEN, THE PIES MAKE THEIR WAY THROUGH THEIR RESPECTIVE "PIPELINE STAGES".

NOW YOU MAY BE THINKING TO YOURSELF "OF COURSE, THE ELEPHANT WILL WIN, LOOK AT HOW BIG HE IS!" BUT THIS DOES NOT TAKE INTO ACCOUNT HIS LONG AND WINDING *INTESTINAL TRACT*.

SOMETIMES *BUBBLES* AND *BRANCHES* GET SHOVED DOWN TO BE DIGESTED. THIS RESULTS IN BURPS AND THE "RUNS", CAUSING A *DRAIN* OF THE ENTIRE PIPELINE, SLOWING DOWN THE PIE PROCESSING.

munch! munch! munch! munch! burp! munch! munch! mumunch!

MEANWHILE, THE MOUSE IS MUNCHING AWAY, STEADILY AND DETERMINEDLY!

I WON!

THE BUBBLES AND BURPS CAUSE DRAINS, BUT THEY ARE NOT AS BIG, SO PIE IS PROCESSED AT A STEADY RATE AND THE MOUSE *WINS*! GET IT?

AH, SURE JON, WHATEVER CHARGES YOUR CAPACITOR...

And so the Techie Godfather's demo has helped Little G4 realize...

I AM NOT A STUNTED SLOW-POKE CHIP! MY SUPERIOR ARCHITECTURE MAKES ME JUST AS FAST, MAYBE EVEN *FASTER*!

THAT'S RIGHT, G4! NOW, TO GET YOU TO THE EXPO! TAP YOUR LEVEL 2 CACHE TWICE, AND YOUR BACKSIDE LEVEL 3 CACHE THRICE...

G4 did what he was told. Suddenly, there appeared a mouse-drawn carriage!

HAVE FUN G4! JUST REMEMBER MOORE'S LAW, AND YOU'LL DO FINE!

...and off to the Grand Expo G4 went!

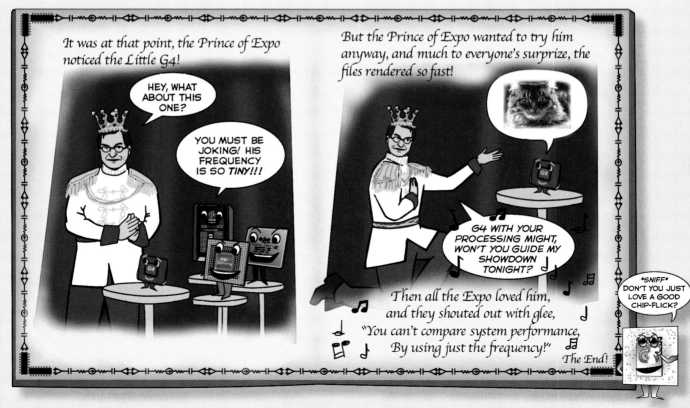

Beware the Ides of MacWorld.

After living his whole life with the classic Macintosh, poor Charlie now found himself trapped in a strange new OS.

Nightmare in Cupertino!

Of course, no one really expected that Cynthia could live up to her last vow.

... if Microsoft had a Genius Bar.

Klingon Pain Rituals

How they cracked Microsoft.

How they code at Microsoft.

Much of the animosity was finally explained by the discovery of Bill's *Despicability Amplification Field.*

Stress Relief Dart Board

For the release of tech-related stress,
brought about by recent Microsoft activity.

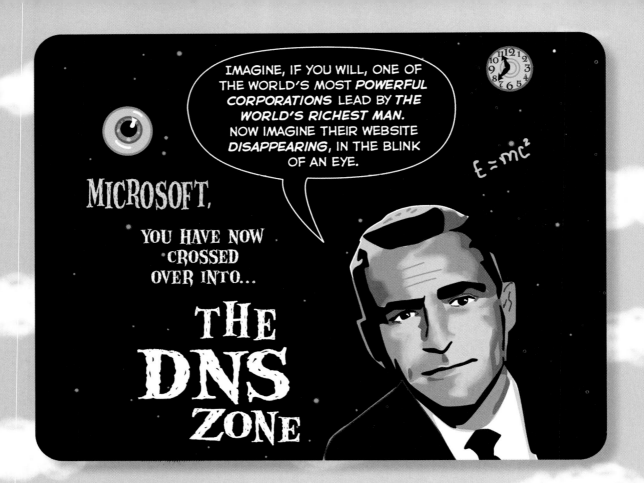

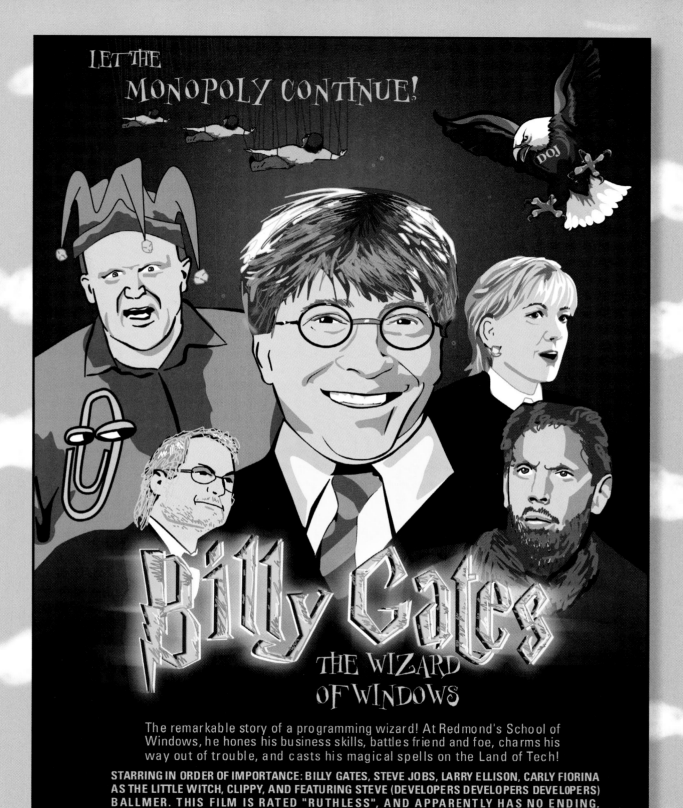

The Force Forecast.

HEADING DOWN TO PLANET EARTH AND CAN'T RESIST BUGGING THE HUMANOIDS? WELL THEN, DON'T FORGET TO PACK SOME OL' FAVORITES!

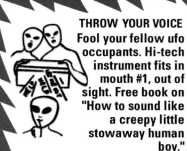

THROW YOUR VOICE
Fool your fellow ufo occupants. Hi-tech instrument fits in mouth #1, out of sight. Free book on "How to sound like a creepy little stowaway human boy."

Slacker Brand HOLOGRAPHIC SELF PROJECTOR
Your Grey Commander will never know you're gone! Just plug in and beam out!

THE CURTA!
Dazzle them with this calculator from the 1950's ... the last time you visited Earth!

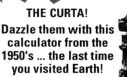

REAL HEAD WIG
Confuse and scare abducties with this wig! They expect aliens to be bald... this will really disturb them!

Homemade "Kooky" T-shirt

Centari IV Abacus User Group

BOOMERANG
The latest in fake-UFO technology. Great for spooking the hell out of lonely desert travellers!

JOY BUZZER
Wear it as a ring, then, when an unsuspecting human offers Peace and Friendship, they'll think you're some kind of "electrical monster"!

MONEY MAKER
Insert a blank piece of paper, turn a knob... and... OUT COMES HUMAN MONEY! You have to fill it with rich humans first, though.

EXHAUST WHISTLE

Just slip it into the eliminator valve of your friend's UFO, then watch him start the ignitorator! He'll think his UFO is exploding and he'll fear for his timestream -- while you roar with laughter.

SECRET SPY SCOPE
Pensize peeper scope for your pouch! No one will ever notice you pulling it out of your pouch and apparently poking yourself in the eye with it.

X-RAY SPECS
Scientific optical principle really works! Put on your "X-Ray" Specs and look at your tenticle! But watch out, annoying human babes will always try and come between you and your tenticle, hoping you'll find their hideous form pleasant in some weird way.

TRICK BLACK SOAP
Looks like an annoying piece of soap, until you use it. Your face is filthy afterwards and you'll look almost human! Even funnier if you can convince a captive human it's "healing food"!

WHOOPEE CUSHION

Place on the chair of someone really important, then watch them scream, and scream, and scream. A scream at keynotes!

SOYLENT GREEN GUM
It's Gum, made out of people, and it tastes bad, for a very long time.

Maybe it wasn't such a good idea to locate a restaurant at the edge of a black hole.

One of the more popular destinations
for time travelling geeks.

Klingon Mac User Group Meeting

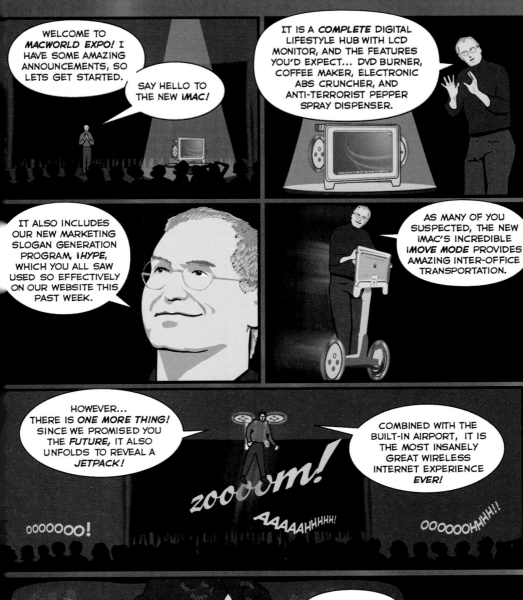

It would be recorded in the geek history books as
The Great MacMania Maritime Disaster.

David Pogue's worst nightmare...
the return of the Missing Manuals!

He always wanted to be a rock star.

The World According to... GEEK!

Keyboard Bitching Session

It was another memorable night at *The Nerd Club*.

It wasn't too long afterwards, that Samantha started blogging someone else.

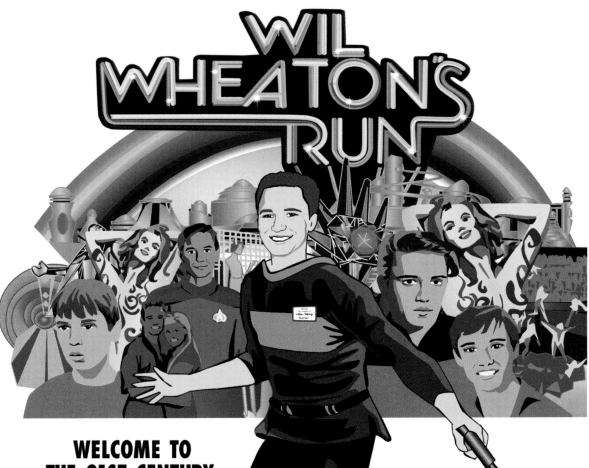

THIS SUMMER, WIL WHEATON TURNS THIRTY!

WIL WHEATON'S RUN

**WELCOME TO
THE 21ST CENTURY.**

Starts July 29th!

**TO BOLDLY BLOG WHAT NO ONE
HAS BLOGGED BEFORE!**

GEEKCULTURE.COM presents A JOY OF T... roduction of "WIL WHEATON'S RUN". Starring WIL (I'M NOT WESLEY) WHEATON . With su... roles by ANNE, NOLAN, RYAN, FERRIS THE WONDERDOG, and a LOGGED-ON CAST OF THOU...DS. Special guest appearance by William Farking Shatner as "The Old Man". Screenplay by 50,00... MONKEYS AT 50,000 TYPEWRITERS. With music by RADIOHEAD, UNDERWORLD, CAKE, AND KLON 88.1. NOW SERVING AT WWW. WILWHEATON.NET.

Support Group for Victims of Internet Service Provider Abuse.

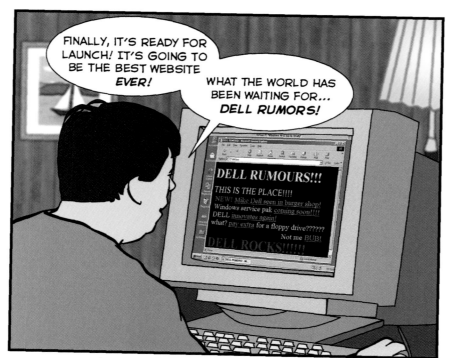

He was about to set a new standard for "Rebel without a Cause."

In a land of wizards, daemons, usrs, and trolls, only one holds the password to absolute power...

THE LORD OF THE ROOT

ONE GEEK TO RULE THEM ALL

Who says girls shy away from math?

Introducing the pop-up Annoying Book Store Clerk.

DREAMERS MAY PERISH...

BUT OUR DREAMS WILL CONTINUE.

JoyWords!

Comments on the Comics and the JoyPolls.

For every Joy of Tech we publish on the web, we create an online poll that relates to the comic. It's a tradition that we started back in early AY2K (After Y2K) days. Initially, it was a blatant attempt to boost our page views, but it soon became a way to compliment the comic, poke fun at the subject matter in a little more detail, and give our readers one more thing. In AY2K's case, the poll also includes an additional comic that added a little something extra to the story. (We've also done that a few times with the JoT.) So, when we thought about what would be included in this book, we realized we couldn't leave the polls out because for us, they are really part of the experience of The Joy of Tech.

We've also included some comments, a little background, or perhaps a geeky tidbit about each comic.

Legend

N: Nitrozac comments.
S: Snaggy comments.

JoyPolls are formatted thusly

Bold: The question.
Plain: The choices.
Italics: The JoyQuips... the sometimes snarky and sarcastic comments on the

JoyPoll choices, viewable only after you have done the poll.

Note that the last result on each poll is reflective of the number of people who didn't vote, but simply "viewed the results."

small text: The "May not add up to's"

BOOT-UP

#373 Your computer on drugs.

S: Our take on the Afroman song "Because I Got High." Hmmm imagine if your computer was a "user." When your computer "got fried" it would have a whole new meaning! N: Now we'll have to do a comic about a computer on the 12-step program.

What's your computer on lately?

Mine's on speed, ... *faster PowerMac, kill kill!* 7%

Mine took a hit of LCD, ... *Laptop in the Clouds with Diodes.* 12%

Mine just sparked up a joy-stick, ... *doesn't that lead to more of the hardware stuff?* 4%

Mine's not on junk, it is junk, ... *how much junk food have you jacked up on lately?* 15%

Mine's going to be high as a Jaguar, as soon as I score me some, ... *no upgrade price? ...god-damn The Pusher.* 30%

Mine's got a buzz off my geekiness, ... *you know I've seen a lot people walkin 'round, with TombRaider in their eyes.* 15%

My computer is in rehab. 13%

May not add up to exactly 100% due to rounding and Joy juice.

#149 Messy Geek.

N: You can take the geek out of the pig sty but you can't take the pig sty out of the geek. This was a very popular comic and I can only hope that it's been printed out and added to the messiest of the messy cubicals out there. S: I recently heard from a fan whose messy co-worker had printed out the comic and added it to his messy geekosphere. While Messy Geek was on vacation, the office conspired to clean up his cubicle. As the finishing touch, they replaced the ink jet version with a framed print of the comic. N: How long before he re-booted his mess?

What do you need most to work your best?

A comfy geekosphere, ... *comfy is relative, although usually away from relatives.* 23%

A quiet space, ... *in space, no one can hear others code.* 13%

All the snacks I can devour, ... *on some days, that number approaches infinity.* 6%

Good ol' caffeine, ... *ever thought about joining Alkaloid Anonyomous?* 15%

A holiday, ... *that sounds so relaxing, can I bring my laptop?* 32%

I need the results. 8%

May not add up to exactly 100% due to rounding and cubiclephobia.

#277 Cutting down to one cup.

N: We were both a little surprised at how much this comic was a hit! Every once in a while I try to give up coffee as I suspect it turns me into a snarling, cornered animal in my cube, but I can't... it's just sooo good. S: Actually, that cup looks just a little bit bigger than some of the ones I use.... GULP! N: I did find a giant cup, perfect for Snaggy, it was big enough for a Newton to swim in, but it was $99!!! S: How much to fill it at Tim Hortons though?

How do you get around your resolutions?

Little by little, bit by bit, I return to my old habits, ... *just do what the rest of us do, return to them all at once.* 13%

I cross my fingers while making them, ... *just so long as you don't cross too many people breaking them.* 2%

I plead temporary insanity, ... *did some of your vices get the best of you?* 4%

Make them so unreasonable as to be unachievable, ... *tell that to Neil Armstrong.* 11%

Do what I do best... blame others, ... *I blame your parents for raising you to do that.* 7%

I just make a resolution not to take my resolutions so seriously, ... *but can you keep that one?* 43%

I'm resolving to vote more this year. 17%

May not add up to exactly 100% due to rounding and resolving differences .

#060 In My Day...

N: This comic is a take on those old lectures you'd get from grandaddy or dad about how they had to endure the agony of walking to school every day in the snow, up hill, etc. Actually when I was in junior high, I really did have to walk 3 miles to school, in the −30 Celcius winter, (with just runners, because I was a silly teen), but it wasn't up hill. It's true!

What does this comic best illustrate?

How things have gotten better since that old fart's day, ... *um, which one do you consider the old fart?* 3%

How Moore's Law also applies to attention spans, ... *ya whatever, on to the next.* 28%

How much I miss those giant Electronic Brains, ... *yep, there were people inside of computers way before Tron.* 4%

How in the future, when that kid is an old man, his grandkids will get really tired of his endless babbling about scooter adventures, ... *well, you gotta admit... a scooter without an anti-gravity pack? BORING!!!!* 31%

How everything is transitory, and life so tenuous, and thank goodness for technology, ... *technology is even more tenuous, but that's life.* 16%

I illustrated that I can view the results. 15%

May not add up to exactly 100% due to rounding and Time being absolute and relative, but never universal.

#260 Meteor Shower

S: Nitrozac and I were watching one of the best meteor storms ever when she came up with this one. Pesky aliens are important characters in our first comic AY2K, and it was inevitable that their counterparts would make an appearence in JoT. N:Those meteor showers are pretty, aren't they? Yeah, but what if they're aliens throwing lit-up bags of poop into our atmosphere? Wouldn't be so pretty, would it? Woz liked this one, being a prankster himself. S: Hey, are you calling Woz a shit-disturber? ;-)

Which alien practical joke bugs you the most?

Fake meteor showers, ... *what's worse is when they create cloud cover during the real ones.* 3%

Continental drift, ... *it's amazing what a little WD30 can loosen up.* 19%

Rainy weekends, ... *that's why they prefer to live in outer space, where there's only the occasional meteor shower.* 18%

All those ones they sell in alien comic books, ... *I always liked the seedy ads.* 14%

I'm a good sport, alien practical jokes don't bug me, ... *they got to you, didn't they?* 30%

I've already been served, man. 13%

May not add up to exactly 100% due to rounding and there being just enough gas in the bag for the bag to burn in the vacuum of space.

#145 The Coffee Cam Tells All

S: When the famous Trojan Room Coffee Machine Cam was finally retired, we thought it would be funny to give voice to the machine's side of things, in a tell-all. I imagine it appearing in a Barbara Walters interview next, a little tear drip running down its side. N:This is the cam that started it all... all those webcams out there owe their beginnings to geeks needing their cuppa joe!

How do you feel about the news of the historic Coffee Cam retiring?

I just filtered it out, ... *it's probably just percolating somewhere inside of you.* 20%

It's grounds to get really upset, ... *so you're boiling mad?* 6%

I just can't stop brewing about it, ... *it's the best way to honor it's memory.* 5%

It's a bitter end, ... *yes, but it was good to last drop.* 37%

Coffee Cams are for drips... *heh, did you see Nitrozac's new coffee maker?* 19%

I savoured the results. 11%

May not add up to exactly 100% due to rounding and Beautiful Joe.

#083 Trolling in a Nutshell

S. It didn't take long for the O'Reilly "Nutshell" series of books to become a geek staple, so we thought to our comic selves, what better Nutshell book than a book about real nuts, Internet trolls. N: Our First Post t-shirt first appeared on a troll doll in AY2K. We designed the shirt to be visible by as many people as possible, which is in the spirit of trolling. Our tests determined it was readable by a normal naked eye from a distance of 120 feet!

What would be your favorite chapter of Trolling in a Nutshell?

How to make Enemies and Influence Newbies, ... *in troll space, everyone can read you scream.* 7%

Trolling for Dollars, Increasing Page Views with Simple Trolling, ... *be careful, one-click trolling is patented.* 6%

Stupid Troll Tricks, ... *troll over and play dead is my fave.* 6%

Advanced Trolling, Creating Your Own New Dumb Saying, ... *Hmmm, here's my go at it... Cold puppet poop, fending for itself. What's yours?* 16%

Everything you wanted to know about First Post, Its Origins, the Legend, Its Uncertain Future, ... *and the obligatory t-shirt link.* 17%

My favorite chapter was moderated down, ... *old trolls never die, they just flame away.* 33%

I viewed the results, along with my troll doll collection. 12%

May not add up to exactly 100% due to rounding and wild blue hair.

ANIMAL Crackers

#140 Battery Park

N: Robots would be great for those with allergies, but I don't know if people would treat them like pets or like toys. Do you take your robot on a trip with you, or just leave it at home unplugged? S: Hmmm, maybe we should market AIBO pet carriers... padded cages with battery backup?

What waste should you clean up?

My computer desktop, ...*I'm pretty sure there's even virtual pizza crusts on it!* 20%

Certain folders of .jpgs, ...*heh, if your girlfriend knows her stuff, she'll find 'em during a dumpster dive.* 24%

The kitty litter box, ...*didn't Billy Joel write a song about that..."don't go changin' to try to please me..."* 12%

My vocabulary, ...*it may be hard re-training your AIBO though, might take a re-boot.* 11%

All my wasted bandwidth, ...*it wouldn't have anything to do with those .jpgs would it?* 22%

I may have just wasted my vote. 8%

May not add up to exactly 100% due to rounding and low batteries.

#292 Cat Protestors

N: This was the first comic we uploaded to sell on our Cafe Press store. It was really just a test, because I had a print file of it handy on my harddrive. But lo and behold it was and continues to be really popular! Who knew? I ordered the mousepad with that image on it, and I really enjoy it, since I don't have a CRT monitor anymore for NitroKitty to sleep on. S: I built a NitroKittyShelf designed to fit behind an Apple LCD display so NitroKitty could sleep on top, but she preferred the good old CRT monitors. Hard to recreate all that luxurious waste heat I suppose.

What effect will the trend towards LCD monitors have?

Lots of cats will be hissed off, ...*it's going to hurt their pride.* 3%

Flat stuff will get super fashionable, ...*that will hiss off a lot of fat cats.* 4%

My office will be a lot cooler, ...*think global, act local, when it comes to warming.* 10%

Throwing rocks at old monitors won't be as fun, ...*there's nothing like the sound of a CRT implosion.* 10%

Cats, unable to soak in heat from CRT monitors, will soak in heat from other sources, thereby causing an ice age, ...*is that why they say "that cat is chillin"?* 31%

I'll be able to pick up lots of great CRTs for cheap, ...*less room on your desktop, but more desktop.* 26%

I pussyfooted around voting. 13%

May not add up to exactly 100% due to rounding and the cat's meow!

#302 Lungfish

N: This comic was a result of some of the crazy patents out there, in particular the one that wanted to patent the hyperlink! S: Hopefully the patent for "the comic" has expired!

What do you claim to hold the patent on?

Hyperlinks, ...*maybe British Telecom needs some Ritalin?* 4%

Biped mobility, ...*put one foot ahead of the other in a Gingerly fashion.* 7%

The stupid question, ...*the stupid answer was ruled a derivative work.* 24%

Geekiness, ...*but patents only cover the useful arts! ;)* 10%

Misery, ...*I thought Microsoft and Morrissey were battling over that one.* 24%

Comics about lungfish, ...*although breathless, they are sometimes like a fish out of water.* 8%

I'm viewing the results, then scooting on over to the patent office. 18%

May not add up to exactly 100% due to rounding and limb-like appendages.

#143: Anthropomorphization

N: The RL model for this cat was a polydactyl (having an extra toe on each foot) stray cat that showed up at our place and spent about a week or two in our garage, until we found it a new home. During that time he was a big hit on the webcam. He must have been a great mouser, with those giant, claw-filled paws. S: NitroKitty had a crush on him, and the two would spend dates staring at each other through the window that separated them. I guess that old "big paws" thing is true.

Anthropomorphization means attributing human characteristics to nonhuman things. What exactly then are the animals in today's comic doing?

Animalmorphization, ...*isn't that some kind of Japanese animation?* 1%

They are anthropomorphized animalmorphizers, ...*I'm pretty sure that is illegal, even in cartoons.* 7%

They are both being really bitchy, ...*well, so would you, it's a zoo in that house!* 34%

Making the biggest mistake of their lives, ...*ya, that monkey's running Windows, and there's a bomb in the pussy's suitcase.* 9%

If I'm not mistaken, that monkey is ambidextrous and that pussycat is polydactyl, ...*gee, no wonder they fell in love!* 36%

I animalistically viewed the anthroprocentric results. 10%

May not add up to exactly 100% due to rounding and pets peeved.

#483 Dr.Phil and the Mad Mad cow.

S: Sometimes I wish there was a Dr. Phil-like race of aliens to slap some common sense into humans. Polluting the planet? Using up all your resources? War? ...How's that working for ya? The Joypoll was...

What could Dr. Phil help you with?

Hardware rage, ... *how's that not working for ya?* 5%

Software Spongiform Bloat-apathy, ... *that can really eat at your brain.* 5%

Mad Programmer Disease, ... *must be the same routines over and over again.* 15%

I'm a real DataQueen, ... *does that mean you overreact to 1's and 0's?* 2%

Slackaholic, ... *it's rather infectious.* 32%

I'm in Denial Of me needing Service, ... *even geeks need optimizing every now and then.* 28%

I didn't want to prion. 10%

May not add up to exactly 100% due to rounding and contaminated relationships.

#285 Kill That Mouse!

N: That's Nitrokitty in the comic. It must seem to cats like we play with the mouse all the time and never kill it. They must be shocked at our cruel entertainment, just batting that thing all day, especially those button-pounder types. You know the type... the people who don't click their mouse, they swat it. *CLICK!*

How long do you play with your mouse?

Just a few minutes a day, ... *wow, thanks for making us such a big part of your mousing adventures.* <1%

About an hour or so a day, ... *only an hour a day, keeps the tendonitis doctor away.* 2%

A few hours a day, ... *so you're more of a keyboard geek?* 19%

Almost every hour in the day, ... *sounds like you're falling into a rat race.* 15%

There are not enough hours in the day, ... *are you a man, or a crazed clicker?* 24%

I prefer other more superior input devices, ... *hmph! Who made you such a big cheese?* 24%

I'm too mousey to vote. 12%

May not add up to exactly 100% due to rounding and toying with the data.

#137 How to Train Your Human

S: The inspiration for this comic was a golden retriever that my mom adopted from a shelter. "Brody" was a rather unmannered doggie and after many problems, she hired a trainer to tame the wild beast. But alas, Brody only succeeded in training my mom. Luckily for all involved, Brody found a new home and soon after, my mom found the perfect dog, Maggie (who apparently doesn't have access to the Internet).

How is a website created by dogs humanly possible?

It was developed by a race of highly intelligent mutant dogs, ... *who let the mutant dogs out?!* 15%

It was developed by a human traitor, ... *he'll be in the dog house if we ever find him.* 19%

It was developed by human double agents, ... *we've had to use dirty tricks against those mutant dogs.* 16%

What Spot Sees is What Spot Gets, ... *does Spot use a Dalmation iMac?* 36%

I barked up the results. 11%

May not add up to exactly 100% due to rounding and dog breath.

The Office Elephant

S. I love this comic, I'm not sure if it's the silliness of the joke, or just the expression of geek glee on the elephant's face. He really looks so excited to be at his new job! N: Yeah, and I bet he'd work for peanuts too! Har har.   You can do the JoyPoll for this comic, ...exclusively for those who have this book! Find it online here...

http://www.joyoftech.com/joyoftech/thebestofjot/index.html

#463 Grooming Time

N: Do you ever look at your cat with envy, as she lounges and grooms herself without a care in the world about deadlines and jobs and other humanly things? S: I look at you that way, Nitro. hee hee.   N: Grrr. I wish I *could* look at you that way. Hee hee hee.

How much time do you have to groom?

I have lots of grooming time, ... *are you being groomed for success?* 4%

I don't have much, but I make time, ... *good groomed geeks get gourmet girls.* 14%

The time between wake up and boot up, ... *wait a second, isn't your computer is always on?* 28%

Nanoseconds, ... *so the comb over is over before the comb is over?* 6%

I have just the right amount of time, ... *so that's why you're looking so good!* 15%

Grooming is irrelevant, ... *you are unBrushed. Prepare to be avoided.* 17%

I'm grooming my computer 12%

May not add up to exactly 100% due to rounding and always a groomsmen, never a groom.

#414 Cat Keyboard Commands

N: One day Nitrokitty walked on our webcam's computer keyboard and it resulted in this strange unknown computer behavior! It took us some time to undo what she had done, (can you say re-start?) We even tried (unsuccessfully) to duplicate it by letting her walk on it again. No luck. Then she repeated the same trick a few days later. We came to the conclusion that NitroKitty knew exactly what she was doing.

What is your pet doing on your keyboard?

Sending secret messages, ... *maybe organizing more of those cat protestors.* 6%

Grazing off all the crumbs and food chunks, ... *so what you are saying is your pet lives with a pig?* 12%

Adding my name to spam lists, ... *or else it's just WORKING AT HOME AND MAKING GREAT MONEY!* 21%

One paw shopping, ... *hopefully it will find the pick of the litter.* 10%

It fell in love with Jaguar, ... *or perhaps some faux Jaguar fur?* 13%

My pet is a geek, it's undoubtedly programming, ... *did it start from scratch, or did you give it BASIC training?* 19%

Pets are my pet peeve. 16%

May not add up to exactly 100% due to rounding and the Personal Electronic Transactor.

Geek Love

#034   I Don't Date Hotmail Addresses.

N: Longtime fan Retropier dubbed this character "Ms. Unattainable" and like many geeks developed a crush on the fiery redhead, ... several even demanded a chance to win her over! I had the idea for the comic from a conversation in our IRC chat rooms. A newbie came into the chat, and flirted with one of the regulars who wasn't receptive, much to my surprise. When asked why, he said, "I don't date unresolved IPs." I thought that was funny, and altered the idea a bit, and there you have it – Ms. Unattainable was born!

What email addresses do you prefer to date?

It's gotta be a .com. 9%

I prefer a nice .org. 17%

I dig a .net date. 13%

Real geeks prefer .edu. 20%

.mil's have more fun. 2%

I've set my sights on a .tv affair. 1%

I'm actually considering dating a snail mail address. 5%

I'll date the results. 20%

May not add up to exactly 100% due to rounding and all the dots I've loved before.

#033 Do you know his history?

N. You can tell a lot from checking someone's browser history! Of course, there's the falsley accused type of history, where porn sites just pop up windows, but still, it all looks quite suspicious. S: I didn't do it! Heh, perhaps it's better to base relationship decisions on Bookmarks and Favorites.

Ever checked your Significant Other's history or cache?

Never! I don't snoop. 26%

Um, well, once or twice I have. 12%

I've tried, but my SO is very efficient at erasing it. 7%

Huh? You mean I can find out where my SO surfs? 2%

My SO is my cache! 28%

I'm just snooping on the results. 22%

May not add up to exactly 100% due to rounding and geek vs geek.

#134 Romeo and Geekiette

N. Yeah, he just wants her for one thing... her kick-ass computer! I can see someone dating someone for their hardware, can't you? You just want to get your hands on their machine, and take it for a spin. I'd call him a Silicon Digger. S: I guess I'm just a hopeless romantic but I like to think he's interested in her software.

Where do the best pickup lines come from?

From Shakespeare... *doth not ye olde classics rock?* 20%

From the X-Files... *just imagine the treasures the spin-off, the Lone Gunmen, will bring!* 15%

From the Geek Love forums ... *all I want is someone who will LOL with me, not at me.* 7%

From well written code... *the "$" really catches the eye.* 30%

What's your sin/cos, baby... *hmmm, is that a trig question?* 13%

I picked up the results. 12%

May not add up to exactly 100% due to rounding and outrageous fortune.

#115 Stressful Breakups

S: There was a study by some sort of Breakup Institute that inspired this comic... although I suspect the data pool was severely contaminated by uptime junkies. N: You know, there are probably thousands of jealous spouses at this very moment as their loved ones are paying more attention to a pile of circuits. –sniff–

Do you find computer crashes more stressful than relationship breakups?

Absolutely, ... *hope you had a pre-boot agreement.* 6%

Absolutely not, ... *does this mean you might give your relationship a boot?* 41%

I've never had a crash, ... *wow, first hour on the computer?* 3%

I've never had a breakup, ... *well, they are kinda like a crash. You try to save what you can, hope you don't have to re-format, and curse yourself if you don't have a backup.* 16%

Tux would never break up with me, ... *a penguin is extremely loyal, set it free, and it will come back to you with all kinds of improved code.* 19%

I love the results. 11%

May not add up to exactly 100% due to rounding and binary breakups.

#144 WiFi Love
N: Another hazard of dating a geek... they've got a two-track mind; hardware and bandwidth! S: Imagine the conversation just prior to the comic... She: Oh Seymour, look at all the lovely lights. He: Wow, think of all the open nodes!

What would you do at Lover's Peak with a date?

Watch The Matrix on DVD on my laptop, ... *that was a drive-in dream date, or was it?* 4%

I'd be on the net, with my date in #babes, ... *how digitally romantic, sort of.* 1%

Spot and identify satellites, ... *watch out for Mir!* 7%

Using my telescope to look at the stars (and the occasional window), ... *think of it as real Reality TV.* 7%

Forget the technology, I'd be all over my date, ... *make sure you use a surge protector!* 65%

I'd take my date up there to view the results. 12%

May not add up to exactly 100% due to rounding and guys with cars getting all the good broadband.

#332 Quantum Girl Watching
S: We love combining extremely cerebral subjects (like physics and technology) with sexy inuendo. We had a lot of fun with that kind of thing and our Techno-Talking Babes of AY2K, and I think this comic captures some of that playfullness. This was the first appearance of Amber, the "flower jeans" girl. Yes, I admit, I had a crush on her for several weeks. Funny how Nitrozac can get jealous of her own drawings sometimes.

What's the sexiest part of quantum physics?

Discreteness of energy, ... *excited atoms are pretty hot.* 4%

Quantum tunneling, ... *hmmm, no one really wants a particle leaking through a barrier do they?* 21%

Particle Spin, ... *angular momentum can be intrinsically sexy.* 5%

Wave-particle duality, ... *not that there's anything wrong with that...* 15%

Heisenberg's uncertainty relation, ... *measurement is always a very delicate process.* 5%

Stop it! I'm getting a Schrodinger, ... *somehow, I don't think your wavefunction is in danger of collapsing.* 31%

I observed the results, and therefore influenced them. 15%

May not add up to exactly 100% due to rounding and organized chaos.

#334 The risks of Linux.
N: You know how some geeks just can't leave work at work? Or they can't figure out why you aren't totally enthralled with something such as a Linux kernel? Well, I guess it beats fighting about the inlaws! S: Nothing beats fighting about the Linux kernel.

What's the riskiest part of installing Linux?

Boring your non-geeky friends to death, ... *whatever, they've died that death a hundred times already.* 14%

Your computer will run better, therefore you'll have to work more, ... *perhaps, but work will have to wait until you're done tweaking stuff.* 7%

You'll soon be drawn into the vicious Vi vs Emacs war, ... *no, it's not related to that Vader Vs Ewoks War.* 17%

You'll be branded The Linux Guy, and other people will bug you to help them install it on their computers, ... *in other words, Geek Heaven.* 27%

You'll fall hopelessly in love with Linux Lass, ... *Geek Heaven version 2.0.* 21%

Risk is what makes being a geek such an exciting personality type. 12%

May not add up to exactly 100% due to rounding and someone pressing Esc.

#127 Predating agreement.
N: That can be one of those little quirks that drive you crazy after a while, maybe even resulting in a breakup – mouse grabbing, especially when you're using a tablet   .
Right, Snaggy?
S. You can grab my mouse any time!

What's on your predating agreement?

No looking at my browser cache or history, ... *and no Norton's un-erase either!* 28%

The right to veto place of date, ... *signaled by me looking at my date, and yelling RUN!* 7%

A music CD and hardware give-back clause, ... *and a non-disclosure sub-clause regarding said collection.* 14%

A "you must visit my homepage" clause, ... *and additional brownie points if you click on my banners.* 3%

No eating food off my plate, ... *if it drops on the floor, it's fair game.* 3%

As long as they have DNA, then I don't worry about an agreement, ... *the aliens on Vega Six will be so disappointed.* 29%

I agree to view the results. 12%

May not add up to exactly 100% due to rounding and not-withstanding clauses.

#444 How to lose a geek in 10 seconds

S: We finally saw the film that this comic satirizes... ouch! Don't you hate it when a movie is so bad it actually hurts you? N: Who's the geek, I bet you thought it was the guy, right? Actually it's the girl! Hee hee.

What tops your list of the most annoying things a Significant Other can do?

Re-organize my computer, ... *especially when it's re-organized right out of the house.* 10%

Forward me spam, ... *hmmm, perhaps it's just a hint to go online shopping together?* 20%

Sign me up for stuff I don't know about, ... *you mean you didn't sign up for a lifetime subscription to the gym?* 11%

Reading my email, ... *even worse though, is they not reading the emails you send them.* 8%

At this point I yearn to be annoyed, ... *yet yearning is so annoying, don't you think?* 23%

Don't touch my mouse, ... *you can't reason with an input device control freak.* 10%

My list is growing daily... *I'll vote later.* 15%

May not add up to exactly 100% due to rounding and my SO dipping into the data stream.

#122 OOPS, He left it all to his Inheritances.

S: My Snaggy-sense tells me that this is comic will soon become a reality. Can't you just see someone leaving money to ensure his Sim community is provided for? N: Yeah, but when they crash, who did they leave it to?

Who is getting your stuff when you die?

Collection Agencies, ... *what's really annoying is their afterlife harassment.* 7%

Government, ... *didn't they take most while you were still alive?* 6%

Smithsonian, ... *um, when they said the Institute, they didn't mean the Smithsonian.* 4%

The Geek Hall of Fame, ... *I'm hoping Bill and Melinda will donate to it.* 5%

Family and friends, ... *oh great, they finally get to clean up your mess.* 35%

I'm taking it with me, ... *does wireless still work six feet under?* 29%

I attended the visitation. 10%

May not add up to exactly 100% due to rounding and Inevitability.

#186 Sim geek.

S: Warning, this comic may seem all too familiar. At least he wasn't spending all his time researching "How to spend more time with your spouse". N: This is a prime example of life imitating computer art. S: Meanwhile somewhere, some place, a wife is leaving her husband because he's spending too much time with his Joy of Tech book.

Where did the geek go wrong?

He shouldn't have been playing games so much, ... *that reminds me... I could use a little perk me up.* 8%

He should just keep playing, and try to get better at it, ... *after all, Life is a game.* 8%

He should have force-quit at the first sign of relationship trouble, ... *TILT!* 11%

Nothing is wrong. Do not adjust your monitor, ... *ignore the cartoonists behind your desktop!* 26%

The cartoon itself is just a Cartoon-Sim, ... *are you sure he's not just watching his webcams?* 34%

I'm viewing my own Sim. 11%

May not add up to exactly 100% due to rounding and relationships with pixels.

#038 Elite Delivery.

S: Don't you think Elite Delivery would be a huge success? N: Yeah, Snaggy also thought Bikini Painters would be a huge success too. Geesh!

What's your favorite fantasy shipping method?

Fem-ex, ... *femme as in female, not as in she-male.* 10%

Courtesan Couriers, ... *they are in the business of pleasing their clients.* 7%

Chip and Dale, the Delivery Guys, ... *also known as the Incredible Hunks.* 4%

What's your favorite fantasy shipping method? (*continued*)

United Babes Parcel Service,... *they deliver, especially in the twin city area.* 21%

The Postmistress General,... *wrap your package well, she can be rough!* 18%

I usually hand deliver,... *shipping alone again?* 22%

I'm all shipped out and just viewing the results. 15%

May not add up to exactly 100% due to rounding and this end up.

#287 The new measure of strength.

N: I like that guy's t-shirt "DumbBells Rock." lol. There was a while, back when spam wasn't as widespread, that geeks would brag about how many emails they get, sort of as a status symbol. Now it means you get a lot of spam, kind of sad, really. S: Now geeks brag about how good their spam filters are!

What is the measure of your strength?

The number of emails I get a day, ... *if you're like me, many are forced repetitions.* 3%

The number of emails I send a day, ... *be careful, you may be overtraining.* 4%

How well I perform my circuit training, ... *can you teach an old computer new tricks?* 4%

How well my computer benchmarks, ... *is that how you got your spec pecs?* 14%

How many pixels I can push, ... *try using an Alternating Mousefinger Curl.* 22%

Only 300 emails? What a sissy, ... *now who's doing the dumbbell shrug?* 30%

I have a variable resistance to voting. 20%

May not add up to exactly 100% due to rounding and alternating dumbbells.

#075 A good provider.

N: Hey, what's she complaining about, he's providing the family with life's one essential necessity! It looks like he hasn't provided much in the way of furniture, other than the computer desk...hmmm. S: Maybe he's a graduate of the Star Trek School of Standing Up at Your Computer.

What do you provide?

I provide junk food and beer processing services, ... *BURP!* 8%

I provide the comic relief, ... *a single joke can breed a billion laughs.* 29%

I'm the bright light in the otherwise dark tunnel of life, ... *are you sure that's not just a train coming?* 24%

I exist to provide providers with someone to provide for, ... *that's fine, provided the providers have enough provides.* 26%

I provided more data in the I Viewed the Results category. 11%

May not add up to exactly 100% due to rounding and the Privy Council.

090 Server Maintenance.

S: Ouch! I can imagine that if his wife heard him say this, his uptime would be severely threatened. N: Haven't you noticed, no matter where you work, there's always the wise cracking sexist guy? S: Not really, I've always worked for myself... DOH!

How many hours of "server" maintenance did you put in?

The entire weekend, ... *and it's still not enough time!* 27%

Just a day or so, ... *absence makes the bandwidth less hogged up.* 7%

Just Saturday night, ... *I guess you haven't fully committed to your server?* 8%

I just phoned in the maintenance, ... *watch out, maybe your server is looking for another sys admin!* 11%

I looked for a server all weekend, ... *there's lots of servers in the sea, have you tried the Net?* 33%

I served myself some results. 12%

May not add up to exactly 100% due to rounding and data being all served out.

#100 Corn Site Collection

S: Who would have guessed corn could be so sexy? No wonder the Green Giant is so jolly! N: To this day Snaggy and I giggle when we pass by signs that say "Fresh Corn." Interestingly, you hardly ever see signs indicating fresh potatoes for sale. S: What about fresh yams?

What's the most annoying thing about corn sites?

Those pesky pop-corn windows, ... *the corn industry leads the way in such jiffy things.* 20%

There's hardly any corn sites for women, ... *if you know of any, I'm all ears.* 5%

I always seem to end up in the queer corn section, ... *not that there's anything wrong with that...* 2%

They always want money before showing me the kernel, ... *maybe you could get the Free Corn Foundation to lobby them.* 37%

I'm sorry, call me a prude, but husking just doesn't turn me on, ... *sure, I bet you're actually suddenly super corned on.* 18%

I husked the results. 15%

May not add up to exactly 100% due to rounding, seed rot and seedling blight.

#121 Geeks Prefer Geeks

S: Geeks get stereotyped in the media as being boring, so we just had to turn the perspective around for this comic. I mean gosh golly, who doesn't find TCP/IP configuration fascinating!!! N: zzzzzz

What's the most annoying thing about non-Net savvy dates?

Their mouth drops open when they are asleep, not while they work, ... *you're kidding! (/me's mouth drops open!)* 4%

They refuse to acknowledge IRC chat as quality time together, ... *and they get grossed out if you say you're going to give them ops.* 18%

When you say 404, they think you're talking about a highway, ... *the lost highway, I guess.* 20%

They will give their credit card out to almost anyone, ... *and sometimes these strangers will take the card away for a few minutes... jeeze!* 8%

When their server goes down, they actually enjoy it, ... *heh, I couldn't resist that one. ;-)* 31%

I like to watch the results. 13%

May not add up to exactly 100% due to rounding and the date from hell.com.

#434 Phallic Fruit

S: A recent scientific study claimed the banana was doomed to extinction due to a lack of genetic diversity... maybe the Doc could prescribe banana Viagra to increase the sex-a-peel? N: Perhaps the banana community could benefit from the great gene pool mixer of online dating!

What's your favorite banana joke?

Why did the banana go to the doctor?, ... *you won't be peeling well either if I tell you.* 3%

Knock Knock. Who's there? Banana. Banana Who?, ... *orange you glad I didn't finish this joke?* 9%

Why did the banana cross the road?, ... *that was no banana, that was a chicken, you turkey!* 3%

Somebody slipping on a banana peel, ... *especially if it's a Freudian slip.* 5%

What's yellow and smells like a banana?, ... *you mean they still haven't cleaned up that monkey vomit?* 13%

Yes, I have no favorite banana joke, ... *well, that's it, I split!* 49%

Banana jokes are doomed to extinction. 14%

May not add up to exactly 100% due to rounding and bananas being berries.

#216 The Big Question.

S: I like the idea of asking our most powerful electronic super computers some of our most human questions. I imagine in the wee hours of the night, between mathematical calculations, super computer geeks may be asking them... I hope so. N: I'm still baffled why Tom Cruise would leave Nicole Kidman!

So, why would Tom Cruise want to break up with Nicole Kidman?

He's totally friggin' nuts, ... *he's the lead actor in Top Duh.* 11%

It was an Impossible Mission, and he accepted, ... *well, let's hope he doesn't self-destruct.* 6%

He fell in love with a super computer, ... *he looked into its Big Blue eyes.* 5%

I'm dating Tom Cruise, ... *that must be a pretty Risky Business, no?* 3%

Who cares? Nicole is now a free woman, ... *free as in beer?* 57%

I drooled over the super computer. 15%

May not add up to exactly 100% due to rounding and teraflops.

#088 Love means never having to move your server.

S: We've seen this happen a few times to couples on the Forums... servers are shared, usr accounts given, but *sigh*, love eventually crashes and needs a reboot. Um, don't forget to change those passwords!

What dangers do your super powers pose to others?

My powers of attraction often make me an unstoppable chick magnet, ... *the attractive force of a chick magnet is approximately proportional to the inverse cube of the distance from the hottie.* 10%

My net surfing abilities can sometimes create white holes of information, ... *perhaps your computer needs an event horizon card.* 13%

My super coding has been known to generate localized text flurries, ... *falling from comma-lus and colon-o-nimbus clouds?* 11%

My remarkable ability to recite user manuals sometimes casts a strange sleeping spell over people, ... *user manuals are some people's kryptonite.* 14%

My super slackerism is surprisingly infectious, ... *you know what they say, monkey see, monkey don't do much.* 39%

My secret identity remains a secret. 10%

May not add up to exactly 100% due to rounding and Brainiac's shrinking ray.

#179 Anniversary Gift

S: This comic is our take on the classic husband blunder of giving your wife the gift of a broom. I did buy Nitrozac a vacuum cleaner recently, but luckily for me she is a bit of a cleaning geek, and loves all the cool accessories. I still have to empty it though. N: If he had given her an iPod, it would have been music to her ears.

So what the heck was this guy thinking when he gave her a modem for their anniversary?

He wasn't, ... *don't worry, she'll probably knock some sense into him.* 23%

He thought that by speeding up his access, his work would be done quicker, then they could spend more time together, ... *yep, studies prove it, get faster access, and you're on the Net less. . . . right. ;-)* 12%

He thought they could spend some romantic nights surfing the web together, ... *yep, surfing was built for two... you and your mouse.* 9%

He wanted her to be proud of his hardware, ... *isn't uptime more important?* 17%

He thought "I need something to get out of this marriage", ... *the mousepad he gave her for Christmas was just the beginning.* 25%

I just noted when my anniversary is. 11%

May not add up to exactly 100% due to rounding and pre-nups.

#343 Auto respond.

S: I'm hoping this comic isn't auto-biographical, is it? N. Yes, dear.

What service do you have on your consciousness?

Auto responder, ... *yes dear reader . . . yes dear reader . . .* 4%

Spam filter, ... *anything that says Geek Culture Webstore is good for the both of us! ;)* 37%

Auto spell checker, ... *its somtine i couwld prbly due wiht.* 11%

Auto signature, ... *that's not your consciousness, it's time to take a shower!* 2%

Auto Forwarding, ... *so it goes in one ear then out the other?* 4%

I'm unconscious, ... *you may need an auto-rebooter.* 27%

I'm receiving the results via eye-mail. 10%

May not add up to exactly 100% due to rounding and Delivery Notification: Data Delivery has been delayed.

#461 Love Text

S: Funny how reading and writing text has once again become such a powerful force in the world of romance. Perhaps this resurgence will produce some of our time's great literature... the 21st century's "Lady Chatterly's emails." N: We've had several couples meet, fall in love, and end up sharing their lives together via geekculture.com. Sometimes I think, what if we didn't do this website... would they still have met? S: Maybe over on ReallySuperFreakyGeeks.com?

What's the moral of this comic?

Sometimes real life isn't as good as the virtual, ... *love is blind, but sometimes anti-aliased too.* 6%

Online personalities are often more interesting than real-life ones, ... *a lot depends on the con-text.* 16%

Geeks will be geeks, ... *you can take the geek away from the computer, but not the computer out of the geek.* 30%

Technology can be sexy, ... *Ti me up baby!* 7%

Laptops rock, ... *especially when brewed with cafe WiFi.* 17%

Even in this age of the image, words are still powerful, ... *l33t!* 9%

I'm still in shock that ShyGeek is going out with CafeChic! 12%

May not add up to exactly 100% due to rounding and mode +i.

#376 If it's too good to be true...

N: When my brother and I were little kids we must've watched a lot of Twilight Zone because we were obsessed with the possibility that we may be just brains in a vat. Which would you rather be, a brain in a vat, or a brain in a skull in real life? S: There's not much difference, is there?

What do you suspect you might actually be?

A brain in a vat, ... *well, if it's a vat of beer, I'm sure you're pretty happy!* 4%

A piece of software, ... *hopefully there's at least some of you that's proprietary.* 9%

A cog in the Machine of Life, ... *at least your not a clog.* 17%

An amoeba having a bad dream, ... *must have been something it phagocytosis.* 11%

A figment of Nitrozac's imagination, ... *or even scarier, a figment of Snaggy's reality.* 16%

I think, therefore I ... *uh, ...hmmmm, ... remember, no matter what you are, there you go.* 24%

My electrodes are unplugged. 16%

May not add up to exactly 100% due to rounding and the rounding simulation.

Hacks and Cracks

#119 Give me your lunch money.

S: This comic sums up the Triumph of the Geek in our technological world, and it was extremely popular. Does anyone feel a little sorry for the former bully though? N: Back in my day you had to take karate and beat up bullies yourself, with your bare hands, none of this fancy-shmancy internet hacking!

Using your geek powers, whom do you like to bully around?

Newbies, ... *such a cowardly act, preying on those least able to defend themselves. ...hee hee.* 7%

Major corporations, ... *ditto, LOL.* 15%

COBOL programmers, ... *haven't they been teased enough?* 8%

I would never use my geek powers for evil, ... *once you go down that path, it will forever dominate your geekosphere.* 54%

I'm the one who tends to get picked on by geeks, ... *not all geeks are such bullies, some even sympathize with lower life forms. ;)* 4%

I was bullied to view the results. 9%

May not add up to exactly 100% due to rounding and the Newbie Defense League of America.

#451 Googling yourself

N: Yet another reason to kiss up to everyone you ever meet... they may post lies and hateful stories about you on their blog and ruin your Google reputation! S: Well, better to have something on Google than nothing at all, isn't it?

How often do you Google yourself?

Never, ... *not even in 10,000,000,000,000,000 000,000,000,000,000,000,000,000, 000,000,000,000,000,000,000,000,000,000, 000,000,000,000,000,000,000,000 years?* 5%

Well, I did once, ... *there's got to be a joke here about googlewacking, no?* 11%

I've done it a few times, ... *hmmm, ever find hair growing on your Palm?* 25%

I google myself a lot, ... *just so long as you don't get too big a google-ego.* 13%

I'm more into Googling others, ... *that's always worth a few Google giggles.* 16%

I just sit back and let others Google me, ... *so does that make you a Google slacker?* 12%

Oh, I thought you were talking about...um, ... *never mind.* 14%

May not add up to exactly 100% due to rounding and the chicken choking while spanking the monkey.

#354 Home in the Range.

S: Wifi is so cool. Nitrozac and I did some wardriving recently, it was such a kick to see the networks pop up as we drove along, looking for that elusive "Password: public." N: ...and another driving hazard was born.

Where would be your dream home?

A home on the WiFi range, ... *I'd settle for Hawaii WiFi.* 12%

A log cabin in the middle of nowhere, with little or no high-tech, ... *cable modem though, right?* 10%

I just adore a penthouse view, ... *no, I didn't mean that Penthouse.* 17%

Keep Manhattan, just give me that countryside, ... *you mean Central Park isn't wild enough for you?* 13%

I'm already in it, ... *there's no place like your home page.* 9%

I'd be happy with root, ... *for now, but one day you'll want to put down some roots.* 18%

I'm checking out cardboard boxes. 17%

May not add up to exactly 100% due to rounding and where your heart is.

#446 Duct tape and cover.

S:In the US, Homeland Security advised Americans to use duct tape in the battle against bioterrorism. .. somebody there must have had a friend in the sticky business. Canadians have known about the wonders of duct tape for years... it's an essential survival tool, and in most Canadian geek arsenals. We have a fan who usually rants about our politcal cartoons... we were pleasantly surprised to get an email from him saying he really liked this one. N: Ok then, we'll let him live another day. ;-)

What is your favorite homemade antiterrorist device?

Duct tape rules, ... *rip, stick, so your eyes won't burn.* 20%

Very large Tupperware containers, ... *a pine box will work almost as well.* 9%

Clothes pegs on the nose, ... *what about the other openings?* 4%

Put a dry cleaning bag over my head, ... *as recommended by the Youth in Asia Department.* 5%

I get the Homeland Security Department to recommend products, then hope the terrorists are crushed in the resulting shopping frenzy, ... *when the going gets tough, the tough get shopping!* 23%

I dig a little hole in the sand and stick my head in, ... *do you draw a line in the sand first?* 21%

I'm shouting "The sky is falling! The sky is falling!" 15%

May not add up to exactly 100% due to rounding and some old cave dweller mumbling on an audio tape.

#020 Geeks got Game

N: Come on, put a crowd of geeks together, equip them with the fastest machines, and how are they NOT going to network game all day? I worked at a design company for about a week, and they definitely had this problem, as they were network gaming from noon on. But, they looked like they were working. Lucky for them I was new, and didn't have the nerve to game instead of work, otherwise they'd have been crying for mercy!

You can do the JoyPoll for this comic, ...exclusively for those who have this book! Find it online here...

http://www.joyoftech.com/joyoftech/thebestofjot/index.html

#433 X never crashes.

S: I always get a kick out of claims that Mac OS X never crashes... OS crashes are like death and taxes. Linux geeks also make the same claims, one of my favorite geek memories is of Nitrozac using the Gimp for the first time... it crashed within a minute! N: Nothing compares to the screaming alarm siren of the overheated chip in our Linux box. Snaggy's nephew was playing a flying sim game for only a couple of minutes and it went off. That was funny, yet terrifying...turned out the CPU fan had fallen off!

What's your favorite OS X urban myth?

It never crashes, ... *that claim reminds me a certain Titannic.* 29%

You can actually hear the kernel popping on those new G4s, ... *it's the ghost of OS Redenbacher!* 11%

There's a hidden program code named "Exorcist" to keep the daemons in check, ... *that's enough to turn your head around.* 13%

If your CPU gets too cold, you get an "Ice" interface, ... *is that why X gets glacial sometimes?* 5%

Quartz Extreme was developed by Timex, ... *so that's why Aqua takes a licking and keeps on ticking!* 8%

If you leave the cover off your Mac, Inkwell will dry up, ... *and if Inkwell dries up, you won't be able to dip your co-worker's pony tail!* 15%

OS X urban myths are urban myths. 16%

May not add up to exactly 100% due to rounding and iRounding.

#462 Killing them software.

S: There was a lot of debate about the issue of killing virtual characters on our forums. N: I think people were having guilt issues when they killed their Sims characters. Weird. Funny, how they probably think nothing of eating meat! I guess we should have 4H programs where you raise prize Sim-heffers and then kill and eat them after, you know, to desensitize us from life's cruel virtual reality. S: Mmmmm, Sim Soy!

When it comes to harming virtual characters, does the thought count?

Yes, the killing of virtual characters is immoral, ... *can they sentence you to the prison of your mind?* 5%

No. Everyone should be free to kill, torture, or perform depravity on their virtual characters, ... *but once you start down the dark path, forever will it dominate your destiny?* 13%

Killing, torturing, and depravation of virtual characters should be limited to those qualified to kill, injury, and deprave, ... *we're all qualified for that, but one hopes we also qualify to not.* 8%

I'd like to see additional killing, torturing and depravity expansion packs, ... *isn't that what they call the Windows Operating System? hee hee!* 29%

I'd rather save, heal, and help my virtual characters, ... *perhaps a Thunderbirds expansion pack?* 10%

I'm going to think about this one a bit, ... *keep an eye out for the thought police.* 17%

I used my mind to view the results 15%

May not add up to exactly 100% due to rounding and somebody torturing the math.

#018 Hacker Con

N: The beauty of being a hacker kid is you're still a juvenile, and therefore you can get away with a lot! S: Perhaps, but there's always a chance someone will get their revenge on you by uploading something personal like the Star Wars Kid video.

You can do the JoyPoll for this comic, ...exclusively for those who have this book! Find it online here...

http://www.joyoftech.com/joyoftech/thebestofjot/index.html

#440 iPhoto Genetic engineering

N: I had this idea when I was watching Steve Job's keynote where he introduced these new retouching features in iPhoto.
S: A picture tells a thousands words, and a little Photoshop hides a thousand days.

What part of you would you iPhoto 2?

Make my wrinkles, freckles, and blemishes disappear like magic, ... *it's a better solution than cutting off your head.* 5%

Color correct those bags under my eyes, ... *don't work on it too long, or you'll get bags under your eyes again.* 7%

Erase a few pounds, ... *oh, so that's how you LOSE 20 POUNDS IN 5 MINUTES!* 20%

Enhance my you-know-what, ... *as long as your you-know-what doesn't get in the wrong hands!* 13%

Revert to Original, ... *you must have been a beautiful baby, but baby look at you now!* 20%

What part of you would you iPhoto 2? (*continued*)

Lets just say my Retouch wand is in for a workout, ... *how many calories do you burn retouching?* 17%

I'm quite comfortable with my big fat geek wedding pictures. 15%

May not add up to exactly 100% due to rounding and red eye.

#076 The Tech Sense

S: People often claim their computer has a personality... but does this spirit carry on after the machine has been retired to Boot-no-more Hill? N: Imagine, you're sitting around the campfire, and then you tell the story of your Commodore 64's ghost climbing up the stairs, creaking in the hall, and slowly opening your bedroom door.... EEEEK! It's PONG! AND YOU HAVE TO PLAY!

Do you believe in computer ghosts?

Yes, ... *and here's the proof!* 12%

No, ... *you mean to say you've never been haunted by bad code?* 8%

No, but I do believe in Computer Hell, ... *um, I said Hell, not H.A.L.* 54%

I'm too creeped out to answer, ... *did you hear the one about the ghost twins? They were just a pair o' normal kind of guys.* 14%

I viewed the results, ... *did you? Or did an unseen mouse click for you.... spooky!* 10%

May not add up to exactly 100% due to rounding and ghosts in the machine.

#077 Technopeasant

S: Of course it's always nice to have your friends and family online, but what is the reality of surfing the Internet together? The horror, the horror!

What's the best thing about techno-peasants?

They're much cheaper to buy presents for, ... *a floppy disk can keep them busy for hours!* 6%

What you do with computers is so mysterious to them, ... *if they did know, would they lose respect for you? ;-)*. 22%

They will never understand your t-shirts, ... *and it is very, very important to have cryptic t-shirts!* 16%

All the more bandwidth for me, ... *you're such a techno-dictator!* 45%

I'm a voting peasant. 8%

May not add up to exactly 100% due to rounding and the vassalage of data.

#030 Full Sized Tetris

S: This comic was inspired by the Technology House geeks at Brown University who created a building-sized Tetris game (http://bastilleweb.techhouse.org/). Woz even played it! We thought it would make great comic material and Nitro came up with the idea of using the perspective of someone inside the building.

How much time have you spent playing Tetris?

Little to none. 14%

A bit. 18%

A lot. 21%

About a thousand years. 4%

One doesn't just play Tetris, one lives it. 27%

I took some time away from Tetris to view the results. 13%

May not add up to exactly 100% due to rounding and infectious Russian music.

#198 Hacker Cards

N: Actually, Snaggy and I did make some Geek All Star cards but alas, it became logistically impractical to mass produce them. So, the tests are ultra-collectible now .   S: One day, maybe not today or tomorrow, but soon, we will make more!

Who would be your most cherished Geek Trading Card?

Captain Crunch, ... *toot toot!* 3%

Woz, ... *OK, a new size TV!* 24%

Steve Jobs, ... *he's not turning gray, he's a Titanium Blonde.* 6%

Linus Torvalds, ... *um, shouldn't it be GNU/Linus Torvalds?* 12%

Bill Gates, ... *there's a joker in every deck.* 2%

Mitnick, ... *I thought he wasn't allowed to be a geek anymore.* 2%

Mafiaboy, ... *he's in Denial.* 2%

Lady Lovelace, ... *a talented geek indeed, but she had a lot of Babbage.* 32%

I'm hoping to get my own card. 12%

May not add up to exactly 100% due to rounding and Geek Gum.

#236 Illegal Juice Use.

N: Nobody ever sent me a secret note written in lemon juice only readable if you played with matches. -sniff-   S: Hint: use a light bulb, not matches! I did try the lemon juice secret note trick once, but just ended up with sticky paper. I think that's how Post It notes were invented.

What's your favorite encryption technique?

Invisible Ink, ... *invisible ink is cool.* 1%

Writing stuff sdrawkcab, ... *01000010 01101001 01101110 01100001 01110010 01111001 00100000 01101001 01110011 00100000 01100110 01110101 01101110 00100000 01110100 01101111 01101111 00100001* 4%

My messy handwriting, ... *so you're using Pretty Gobbledygook Penmanship?* 60%

Anything with a backdoor, ... *oh, kindly close it on your way out, so the bugs don't get in.* 4%

I have no secrets, pretty much anyway... *heh, you don't now, thanks to that backdoor. ;)* 15%

I'm spying on the results. 12%

May not add up to exactly 100% due to rounding and holding a candle under it.

#432 Mitnick's First Surf

S: We had a lot of fun with this comic, and it was really neat when the Screensavers TV show picked up on it and reported it. Funny seeing Leo and Patrick report on our Leo and Patrick comic. A week later they fulfilled their cartoon destiny by broadcasting Kevin Mitnick's first surf live on the show. N: Yep, it pretty much went exactly as we had scripted.

Where is the first place you'd surf after five years?

I'd check my email, ... *hope you had a good spam filter!* 15%

Nudie pictures, nuff said, ... *naked people haven't changed too much lately.* 12%

I'd head over to the Internet Archive and try to catch up slowly, ... *time waits for no one, while you're catching up, you're missing more!* 3%

I'd catch up in the Joy of Tech Archives, ... *so much Joy, so little time.* 16%

Go to all my old favorites... log into eWorld, get the latest version of CyberDog, check out HotBot, go to Pets.com, then some Napster, ... *but will it all fit on your floppy?* 17%

After five years away, I'd hope I'd be cured, ... *cured as in epoxy resin?* 22%

I don't surf, I just whistle into the phone. 13%

May not add up to exactly 100% due to rounding and sledghammering.

Girls! Girls! Girls!

#189 Very powerful System

N: Another work hazard, someone finding out that you use the company's T1 line, super fast, super huge storage computer for your own sick thrills. Like me, ... I'd die if Snaggy saw my "cute kitten pics" folder. S. Yeah, um, ... I have one of those too. *Cough*

What do you really use your powerful system for?

Um, work, ya, lotsa work, ... *you're currently working as an Official Cartoon Inspector.* 14%

Games, ... *is that why you call them your toys?* 5%

Getting tunes, ... *downloading music is fun, but hopefully you don't forget about the key of Life.* 2%

Acquiring dirty pictures, ... *nothing is cleaner than a bunch of 1's and 0's.* 2%

All of the above and so much more, ... *you mean, you even Punch the Monkey? *gasp** 35%

I use my non-powerful system for all of the above, ... *hey, if it works, cherish it.* 26%

My non-powerful system can't vote. 14%

May not add up to exactly 100% due to rounding and using powerful systems to order t-shirts.

#448 The Employer

N: Don't you just abhor the dreaded search for employment? It's hard to not act like a totally desparate brown noser when you're looking for a job too. But at least with a show like this comic, you'd actually get something in return instead of a big goofy guy with a rose and ball and chain. S: A paycheck with a ball and chain?

What would be your favorite scene of The Employer reality show?

The part where The Employer weeded out the field by making the prospective Employees eat at the company cafeteria, ... *oh my, these reality shows have gone too far!* 7%

The shocking episode where the Employees were subjected to surprise drug testing, ... *ahhh, so that's why that guy was peeing in his cubicle?* 13%

The spectacular Fantasy Business Trips, ... *the look on their eyes when they received the company credit card... priceless.* 6%

The scenes where the finalists had The Employer back for dinner with their families, ... *but I thought that ancient tradition was extinct!* 3%

That dramatic business card ceremony where one Employee rejected the Employer's offer, ... *he must have gotten a better offer from The Entreprenuer.* 22%

The hilarious outtakes from the Simulated Office Party, ... *that scene was filmed just before the surprize drug tests.* 30%

This reality show is too realistic for my tastes. 15%

May not add up to exactly 100% due to rounding and downsizing.

#064 Job Description

S: Hmmm, I don't think we have one of these people working at Geek Culture head-quartes, do we? N: OK people, you heard the man! Go to our website! Join our forums! Buy stuff! Hee hee.

What's your real job description?

The one who is indispensible, ... *but just try and tell that to the dispensibles.* 13%

The one who does it all but receives no credit, ... *huh? I thought some other guy had that title!* 24%

The one who does nothing but receives all the credit, ... *so you're a zero hero?* 5%

The Ultimate Slacker, ... *well, at least you're motivated to achieve perfection in something.* 21%

I'd like to apply for any of the above, ... *descriptions often sound better than the real job.* 22%

I am the one who views the results. 12%

May not add up to exactly 100% due to rounding and butts in the gears.

#048 All the Rage

N: Being in charge of normal profits would be maddening enough, but online profits? That's rage. S: If you are so concerned, then why would you inflict such cartoon suffer-ing on that poor comic character?   N: Because we of this reality find their cartoon suffering to be funny.

What sets off your rage?

Tech stock drops, ... *well, at least you had something to lose.* 7%

404 File not found, ... *look at it this way, at least the server's still up.* 26%

Somebody ate all the cookies, ... *in the short term anyway, cookies are not a finite resource.* 18%

Computer problems, ... *raging against the machine again?* 15%

The Master didn't send me the Enigma, ... *he's no longer on my Christmas list either.* 20%

I viewed the results... *try not to get too enraged, they are just results.* 11%

May not add up to exactly 100% due to rounding and infuriating anger management classes.

#305 Fullfilment

N: I had the idea for this comic from reading the Dalai Lama's book about achieving hap-piness. Somehow I couldn't get the picture out of my mind of the Dalai Lama in our culture, looking for a job. Now, I noticed that he released a book about achieving happi-ness at work. Which is kinda funny because he doesn't really work, he meditates   . S: Hey! It's tough work being peaceful!

So why would the Dalai Lama want a job in the first place?

He wanted to feel your pain, ... *hopefully he made you forget some pain, with a chuckle.* 6%

He didn't want to be known as the Lazy Lama, ... *I'm not lazy, I'm meditating!!!* 3%

He answered a spam email "Make great money from your Temple!", ... *Free your country from oppression NOW!* 15%

He was just Monk-eying around, ... *he's got such an en-chanting sense of humor.* 4%

He's got this really bad eBay addiction, ... *he keeps bidding on artifacts from his former lives.* 11%

He didn't really go there for a job, but he is just too nice to say no, ... *at least he doesn't have a holier-than-thou attitude.* 43%

I peacefully resisted voting. 14%

May not add up to exactly 100% due to rounding and compassion for data oppressors.

#102 The Entrepreneur

N: Talking about online profits, isn't eBay the only company that did it? Funny. Oops! Gotta go, I have to snipe that 1940's dynamite igniter! S: I gotta go too... must organize those gold ingots! N: The chocolate ones?

What would you sell on eBay?

My coin collection, ... *isn't that where the term "mint condition" was coined?* Less than 1%

My stamp collection, ... *you'd probably take a licking.* 1%

My comic book collection, ... *I hear Marvel has cut their print runs, better buy up now! (This message brought to you by Marvel Marketing)* 6%

My AOL floppy disc collection, ... *just imagine the look on your grandkid's face when the appraiser on "Antique Road Show" tells them how much it's worth!* 61%

My animated gif collection, ... *even rarer, your animated jpg collection.* 13%

I sniped the results. 16%

May not add up to exactly 100% due to rounding and bidding on your own junk.

#193 Office Candy

N: Ever been so hungry that those rubber feet look actually tasty? S. Not really. I've only been hungry enough to chew on my pencil eraser.

Of these, which is your favorite candy to nibble on?

Jube Jubes, ... *aka Ju-Jubes, can be deadly when thrown at unsuspecting target.* 2%

Suckers and lollypops, ... *or perhaps a tootsie roll?* 4%

Just about anything made of chocolate, ... *come on now, I don't want to hear any Snickers out there.* 32%

She works at a nightclub I frequent, ... *you don't mean the Kit Kat Club do you?* 37%

My pencil's eraser, ... *the end of a pen will do in a crisis though.* 5%

I'm nibbling the results. 16%

May not add up to exactly 100% due to rounding and blackballs.

#158 I've got worms

S: Funny how for such piles of silicon, our computers are always getting such carbon life-form diseases... bugs, viruses, worms... illegal operations.

What's the worst infection your computer has had?

A worm, ... *most don't look as good as Anna Kournikova.* 1%

A virus, ... *I guess you were just looking for love notes?* 3%

A trojan horse, ... *beware of geeks bearing attachments.* 1%

A Microsoft product, ... *oh Mr. Gates, you know I'm just kidding, don't you?* 71%

A newbie, ... *they are persistent little devils, but eventually they mature and move on to their own host.* 15%

I viewed the hermaphroditic results. 7%

May not add up to exactly 100% due to rounding and night crawlers.

#298 Genius George

N: At Linux World Expo, I was sitting in the lobby and listening in on a group of marketer drones. It was one of those moments where you have to hold yourself back from jumping on the coffee table and screaming, "You're such a mumbo jumbler, you don't even know what you're saying!" S: But would they have listened to you, being a girl and all?

So, what is the moral of this comic?

Beware of coworkers stealing your ideas, ... *but aren't you part of the Collective?* 5%

Impress the boss, not the girl, ... *unless the boss is a girl.* 7%

Real Geniuses keep it simple, stupid, ... *but I bet they don't KISS the girl.* 44%

To make money, you have to spend money, ... *on that note... go make a million!* 1%

Bosses take you more seriously if you drink coffee, ... *even more if you bring them a coffee.* 14%

Green dresses are bad luck at the office, ... *that's not a real green dress, that'd be cruel!* 10%

Capitalistic comics are immoral. 15%

May not add up to exactly 100% due to rounding and green text.

#139 Forehead ads

S: Nitro wanted to start a business selling corporate logo tattoos on celebrities for years now, but this is the closest we've come to that. N: This is a great marketing idea! Except for hermits, they wouldn't get much traffic.

What part of the body gets the best flick-throughs?

The forehead, ... *crushing their heads doesn't count.* 7%

The chest, ... *is it the Medium or the Message?* 14%

The back, ... *I've noticed the KICK ME company buys a lot of back ad space.* 2%

The bum, ... *just don't make an ad out of yourself.* 30%

I'm not sure, but I hate those pot-out ads, ... *you mean they don't appeal to an older demographic?* 32%

I clicked the results. 11%

May not add up to exactly 100% due to rounding and monkeys punching back.

#352 Mybossisanidiot.com

N: I've had bosses that would definitely deserve this kind of honor and distinction. Unfortunately I had to express myself the luddite way, ... bad mouthing them all over the place. Alas, it sort of had the same result that Stanley got, hmmmm.

What would be your favorite section of MyBossisanIdiot.com?

The boss ranting forums, ... *well, since we brought it up, you may as well have a go.* 7%

The "My Boss Sux!" e-cards, ... *the virtual burning paper bag full of poop is the most popular.* 3%

The where-is-your-boss-now Boss-Cams, ... *yes, but who's watching the watchers?* 35%

The pin-the-tail-on-the-ass game, ... *that's not a tail.* 14%

What would be your favorite section of MyBossisanIdiot.com? (*continued*)

The "I am a boss" confession booth, ... *Ok, fess up!* 7%

The spin off site, My-Employees-are-total-Idiots.com, ... *well, we all work for somebody else in the long run.* 15%

I'm too afraid my boss will find out I voted. 15%

May not add up to exactly 100% due to rounding and rightsizing.

#299 Stupid Stupid Stupid

S: This is one of those stupid stupid stupid comics that for some reason a lot of people found funny... is it because at some point in their lives, everyone doesn't know what ethernet is? N: Or maybe because at some point everyone's accidentally pulled theirs out?

So, what do you think happened next?

Blue Shirt Guy explained what ethernet is to Coffee Holding Guy, ... *over a nice warm cup of 10Base Tea.* 2%

Blue Shirt Guy didn't know, so he and Coffee Holding Guy looked it up on the net, ... *so I guess he got he got his ethernet cable plugged back in.* 5%

Blue Shirt Guy did the "stupid stupid stupid" routine to Coffee Holding Guy, ... *so in other words, he did a crossover?* 20%

Coffee Holding Guy suddenly became known as Coffee Spilled All Over Himself Guy, ... *he was lucky he didn't get it interface.* 39%

Bob Metcalfe just happened to be walking by, so he explained it to them, over a coffee, ... *it was one of those ethereal moments.* 17%

I'm lagging a bit. 14%

May not add up to exactly 100% due to rounding and quasi-rigid luminiferous ether.

405 Dress for Success

N: The good thing about working at home is you can pretty much dress as you please, although sometimes your self-esteem will pay for it!

What do you not have the energy for anymore?

Work, let alone dressing for work, ... *you might raise the energy level at work if you go undressed.* 30%

The social scene after work, ... *if you mean IRC and chat, you really should be doing those during work hours.* 12%

My email, ... *hmmm, while you were doing the poll, you may have got one... better check. ;)* 12%

Relationships, ... *hmmm, while you were doing the poll, you may have lost one, better check!* 11%

What do you not have the energy for anymore? (*continued*)

Hanky Panky, ... *easy come, easy go.* 7%

I'm the Energizer Bunny, ... *keep on clickin'!* 13%

I was exhausted by the choices. 12%

May not add up to exactly 100% due to rounding and self-entropy.

#417 Take a Dayoff

N: Don't you just hate it when some idiots are really sick and they go to work anyway knowing they were sick and exposing people to the virus? Why??!! So they'll impress their boss? Geesh! S: They are probably just under mind control of the viruses... GO TO WORK... SPREAD US THROUGHOUT YOUR SPECIES... TAKE US TO YOUR LEADER!

Which medicine do you wish Dr. Nitrozac would prescribe you?

DayOff, in large doses, ... *just don't settle for the generic AfternoonOff.* 9%

CareerChange, ... *sometimes CareerChange is as good as aRest.* 10%

ExtendedVacation, ... *warning, ExtendedVacation can produce the unwanted side effect of BeingReplaced.* 19%

iQuit!, ... *do not use while operating machinery, including chainsaws, steamrollers, or electric scissors.* 8%

MotiVation, ... *sometimes sold as Brown Nasel Spray, the suck-up-to-the-boss-to-get-ahead medicine.* 22%

Laughter is working for me, ... *take three JoTs a week, do the JoyPoll, and tell me about it in the Forums.* 18%

I don't do virtual drugs, but will take the results. 10%

May not add up to exactly 100% due to rounding and data-congestion.

#295 Geek Olympics

N: Come on, admit it, you started cheering like a madman when you saw the winning parcel arrive at the Cross-Country Package Tracking destination, didn't you?

What's your favorite Geek Olympic sport?

The Mouse Marathon, ... *isn't there a movie about this... RollerBall?* 4%

The eBay Sniper, ... *this one takes geek-like reflexes.* 17%

The Decafe-alon, ... *that sport would give me a headache!* 6%

Freestyle Carpal Tunnel Syndrome, ... *quote the gold medalist writer... "My note is legal tendon."* 15%

Pong Deathmatch, ... *gentlemen, choose your paddles.* 28%

What's your favorite Geek Olympic sport? (*continued*)

The Extended Couch Potato, ... *the only event where potato chip doping is not frowned upon.* 15%

I'm waiting for web surfing to be officially recognized. 12%

May not add up to exactly 100% due to rounding and artistic marks over technical merit.

#054 Geek Whisperer

N: Working in a cube farm is like living in a barnyard, isn't it? Just a sec, someone came in to muck out my stall. S: Time to put you out to pasture, methinks.

What tames or calms you down?

A night off work, ... *or does not working make you worse?* 8%

My pet, ... *animal, human, Sea Monkey, or Personal Electronic Transactor?* 9%

Comics have been known to help, ... *hmmm, they often add to my stress level. ;-)* 22%

The right kind of ingested substance, ... *we're talking donuts here, right?* 22%

I am UNTAMEABLE! Oh, I gotta go, my _____ is coming, ... *yep, those _____'s sure can be _____!* 20%

I'm wildly viewing the results! 16%

May not add up to exactly 100% due to rounding and sweet nulls whispered in your ear.

#183 Root Problem

N: Personally, I think this geek just thinks he's like Neo in the Matrix, and he's trying to get out of his goo pod. S: Hmmm, what is the root password to my goo pod?

So, what would drive you out on a ledge?

Forgetting my passwords, ... *have you tried "password"?* 3%

The fresh air and exhilarating view, ...*it goes by quick at g=10m/s!* 30%

A couple of AI's hunting me down, ... *just don't drop the phone, Neo.* 25%

A Giant Homer, ... *you knew I meant the breed of pigeon, right?* 8%

Someone out there needing rescuing, ... *especially if they have the root password!* 19%

I watched the results jump. 12%

May not add up to exactly 100% due to rounding and acrophobia.

#264 Speaking in Spammish

N: What's even more fun is reading the fake names of the senders. S: It's not when a spammer has spoofed your email address, and you're reading spam from yourself!!

What's your favorite Spammish phrase?

TEENS TEENS TEENS, ... *those were such awkward years, weren't they?* 14%

Earn a Living Online, ... *lol. ;)* 4%

Boost Windows Reliability, ... *now there's an oxymoron!* 24%

Findout About Anyone Fast Now, ... *then think about why you care.* 6%

Attract women - through science, ... *I recommend using your brain, not natural herbal Viagra phermones.* 19%

The Amazing Power of Bulk Email, ... *to irritate and annoy.* 13%

I'm filtering the results. 16%

May not add up to exactly 100% due to rounding and the Hottest Online Business Opportunity of the Century!

#340 Brute Force Compactor

S: Is it a cartoon crime when virtual characters try to kill off other virtual characters? Or maybe he is just trying to crush a cell phone. N: He's not killing, he's recycling!

Which tech ad character would you like to compact?

Verizon's "Test Man", ... *if he's compacted and no one hears, does he make a sound?* 1%

Steven the Dell Dude, ... *maybe you could Compaq him?* 35%

IBM's Codernauts, ... *they are programmers from a parallel universe, looking for software... just write it!* 2%

Those flying Windows people, ... *you may have to wait until duck hunting season opens.* 10%

Jeff Goldblum, ... *and I thought Macs weren't supposed to have viruses.* 1%

All of them could use some Brute Force, ... *crush, crush, crush their heads!* 32%

I'm in a dead spot. 14%

May not add up to exactly 100% due to rounding and the data being dropped.

Techie-daze

#086 Housecoat Day

N: Wearing a housecoat to work says, "I'm so busy working, I don't even have time to take care of my appearance." Isn't that the ultimate in dedication? Aren't these the hardest workers, the slobby looking ones? This comic is for them. May they wear their housecoats with pride!

What's your favorite National day?

National Stay in Bed Day,... *cancelled, since no one came to the opening ceremonies.* 28%

National Caffeine Appreciation Day,... *sometimes known as National Coding Day.* 16%

National Go Home Early Day,... *every 7 years, it lines up with National Go to Work Late Day.* 15%

National Slap Someone on the Side of the Head Day, ... *also known as National Three Stooges Day.* 21%

National National Day Appreciation Day,... *what about a National Night?* 9%

I celebrated National Poll Results Day. 8%

May not add up to exactly 100% due to rounding and fuzzy slippers.

#489 Far Far a Father's Day

N: Sometimes I think about what if in the far future when future anthropologists are digging through the ashes and dust of long lost civilization and they come across the only intact artifacts of our times – Hallmark greeting cards. They would think we live in a completely Utopian society! I think there's a niche market for cards for those who'd like to really express how they feel.

What would be your favorite Star Wars greeting card?

Evil Bastard Father's Day, ... *was Fat Bastard's dad evil too?* 7%

Congratulations on finding your twin, ... *maternal, paternal, fraternal, polar body, or conjoined?* 3%

I love you! I know, ... *celebrated concurrently on I'm-not-scruffy-looking Day.* 13%

I'm sorry for your Death Star loss, ... *a touching show of support for all those innocent Death Star II contractors' families.* 17%

Sorry your boyfriend went all evil on you, ... *and you had to hide the kids, and flee to a far away planet.* 15%

Happy Ewok Hunting Day, ... *is that like Dog Shooting Day?* 30%

I'm more of a Star Trek cards person. 12%

May not add up to exactly 100% due to rounding and Millenium Falcon Bug.

#037 Techie Day

N: I was helping Snaggy fill out his census form and there was a space for his religion. I wrote "Star Trek." At first he laughed, but then he realized it was true. Heh heh.

How did you spend National Techies Day?

Shining a spotlight on this country's workforce development challenges by creating national awareness of technology issues and facilitating dialogue between leaders in government, industry and education leaders to determine steps for solutions, ...*um, ok. Are donuts and coffee involved in this somehow?* 4%

Promoting techie goodwill, ... *root unto others as you would have root do unto you.* 4%

Slacking off, as usual, ... *I don't consider watching AY2K animations slacking off!* 26%

Slacking off a little more than usual, ... *this was the easiest poll choice, wasn't it?* 54%

I'm viewing the results, ... *which counts as working.* 10%

May not add up to exactly 100% due to rounding and techie technicalities.

#169 Ears First!

N: Ears first for me. That's after the eggs are gone. S: Ditto. I do like to anesthetize the bunny in the freezer first though.

How do you like to eat your Easter bunny?

Ears first, ... *some say it is the most humane method, as the bunny can't hear you coming for the second and third rounds.* 31%

Feet First, ... *"save the best for last", but by then, aren't you sick of chocolate?* 2%

I start in the middle, ... *this approach was first suggested at the Camp David summit.* 10%

I'm an easter-bunny-itarian, ... *to each his own... (all the more for me!)* 12%

This subject is just way too controversial, ... *I suppose you're one of those Tail First fanatics?* 32%

I'm still working on my Christmas candy. 10%

May not add up to exactly 100% due to rounding and the need for a big glass of milk.

#291 Groundhog Day

N: Recently on the CBC news, they broke a story about Wiarton Willie "murdering" two other albino ground hogs in their den. I think he played too many video games and became violent, and thought the other groundhogs were aliens in corridors.

S: That's one thing I love about Canada, a scandal involving a weather-forcasting albino groundhog will be the lead story on the National news.

What do you like to check before going to work?

The weather and/or the traffic, ... *they have a symbiotic relationship.* 7%

My email, ... *you have a symbiotic relationship with it perhaps.* 33%

I check to see if my website's still up, ... *is that a reflection of your ego or your id?* 5%

I check to see if any of my stuff got stolen, ... *I think it's time to update your burrow.* 4%

My pulse, ... *well, it's always a good sign if you can check.* 30%

I check my goldfish, my ant farm, and my Sea Monkeys, ... *and you trust them enough to leave them at home alone?* 6%

I'm just checking the results. 12%

May not add up to exactly 100% due to rounding and forgetting the checklist.

#253 CEO costumes

N: Snaggy and I had a really fun time carving faces of famous geeks onto pumpkins then watching them morph and shrivel over time. The best was Ellen Feiss, she was very pumpkingenic.

S: It was kind of sad though, two weeks later, having to toss out the rotting remains of geek vegetables.

Who's the scariest CEO?

Steve Jobs, ... *he's only scary if he doesn't like something you've done... *GULP** 3%

Jeff Bezos, ... *I've always been scared by clowns. hee hee* 1%

Steve Ballmer, ... *he's Frankengates' Monster.* 28%

I'd make case, for Steve Case, ... *is he responsible for that nightmare... "The AOL Freebees that Devoured Netscape"?* 4%

It's Bill Gates, ... *apparently, when Satan dies, he's going to Redmond.* 25%

It's me!!! Bwahahahaha, ... *attention Steve, Jeff, Ballmerman, Bill, and Mr. Case, could you please stop voting for yourselves.* 8%

CEO's aren't that scary, ... *but those investor Goblins can be!* 13%

I was too scared to vote. 14%

May not add up to exactly 100% due to rounding and I got a rock.

#402 Pirates of Silcon Valley

N: Remember those "Tots" episodes in super hero comics? Imagine a Tots Joy of Tech: Little Woz: "Hey pals, I got lots of candy for everyone, enjoy!" Little Jobs: "My candy is phenomenal, and one more thing...". Little Gates: "Hello, I'm assimilating your candy."

So how do you think the night ended up?

The Woz kid got arrested for pranks, ... *he is such a phreaky tyke.* 3%

The Jobs kid convinced the parents to give them all their candy, ... *not only that, they felt amazing doing it!* 8%

The Gates kid got teased a lot, ... *awwww, poor little billy-ionaire.* 5%

The kid dressed as Linus taught them all to make their own candy, ... *he was later labeled Public Enemy Number One by the local chocolate factory.* 13%

The Gates kid got teased a lot, but ended up with most of the candy in the neighborhood, ... *and the following year he resold it back to the parents.* 40%

Dad had the most fun playing the big bad wolf, ... *so he got the trick and the treat?* 19%

I wouldn't mind if she handed out Apples. 10%

May not add up to exactly 100% due to rounding and shell out commands.

#413 Klingon Turkeys

N: This holiday season I'm going to try Tofurky. That would be very Vulcan. S: I tried it last year... it was... fascinating, but it cost so much I'm sure I must have bought it from a Ferrangi!

What is your favorite Thanksgiving battle cry?

What is your favorite Thanksgiving battle cry?

To boldly go where no gravy has gone before, ... *we have engaged the butterball.* 3%

Turkey is a dish best served cold, ... *in the original Klingon.* 10%

Resistance is futile. Prepare for my appetency, ... *it was later known as the battle of Wolf-down 359.* 7%

Pumpkin pie, the Final Frontier, ... *burp it up, Scottie!* 12%

The needs of the many outweigh the lives of the poultry, ... *it is more logical to enjoy a tofu turkey with Spock.* 25%

It's overdone, Jim, ... *he's a doctor not a baster!* 29%

Eat long, then pass out. 12%

May not add up to exactly 100% due to rounding and Red Cranberry Alert.

#421 First Interview

N: Later in Barbara Walters' life she would be interviewing a sluttly white house intern, washed-up, drugged-out actors, and producing a show of clucking gossipy women discussing the trivialist of matters. Is she bitter?

So, once again, you find yourself doing the JoyPoll. Are you bitter?

Yes, I'm terribly bitter, ... *bitterness is a dish best served with pizza and beer.* 9%

I'm just sort of numb-to-the-world bitter, ... *and the choir sings "Numb to the world..."* 17%

Not at all, for it's better to have voted and laughed, then never JoyPolled at all, ... *sure, that is until your JoyPoll chad gets dimpled or pregnant.* 19%

I'm too sweet to be bitter, ... *mmmm, chocolate JoyPoller!* 6%

This is my first JoyPoll! I'm very excited, ... *I hope it was good for you!* 3%

I'm not bitter, I just don't believe in Barbara Walters, ... *wait a second, hold on now, is that a tear in your eye? Zoom up!* 34%

I'm bitter about the poll choices. 8%

May not add up to exactly 100% due to rounding and the North Magnetic Pole.

#428 New Year's Resolutions

N: Forum member Rednivek had a crush on Janie Porche, the girl in the Apple Switcher ads who "saved Christmas." S: He wanted her to save Hanukkah!

If you were the aliens, what would you do?

Fire the planet evaporator, asap, ... *are you the one who turned the Planet Oort into a cloud?* 9%

Selectively fire the evaporator, ... *make sure you set it to evaporate local, not global.* 18%

Definitely wait until MacWorld Expo is over, ... *hopefully you won't have post-keynote depression.* 22%

Make a resolution never to use the planetary evaporator, ... *you could try a planetary juicer, but they are so hard to clean afterwards!* 3%

Try to sell the evaporator to Uncle Owen, ... *but Uncle Owen needs vaporators, not evaporators!* 6%

Spend New Year's on Moon Babe Alpha, ... *it's a typo on the Space Map, but Moon Base Alpha doesn't want it fixed since they get more visitors that way.* 26%

I'm alien to voting. 13%

May not add up to exactly 100% due to rounding and in space, no one can hear you sublimate.

#429 MacWorld Eve

S: MacWorld Expo is like Christmas morning for many Mac geeks, oooo the excitement... so tempting to peek at the rumor sites, the drama of trying to log onto the Quicktime stream, and the thrill of the "one more thing." N: Followed shortly by anger management when you realize any new hardware is completely out of your league financially.

What's your favorite MacWorld Expo Eve tradition?

Tracking the rumors, ... *but be careful what you track in.* 20%

Updating my Quicktime, ... *prepare for streaming... Engage!* 10%

Making keynote wishes upon my Computer Angel, ... *you never know, there's always a little Reality Distortion in the air this time of year.* 4%

Leaving out some carrots for ol' Saint Steve, ... *and maybe some fresh meat for Jobbie the Jaguar?* 4%

Laying down the rules for my keynote drinking game, ... *when Steve takes a drink, you take a drink. Demo, shot of whiskey. Showdown, guzzle a beer. Computer freeze or bug, double it up.* 14%

It has to do with Lust Factor 10, ... *and if you play the drinking game first, your partner will look like a 10.* 25%

I'm practicing my Steve heckling. 19%

May not add up to exactly 100% due to rounding and a Soviet Sputnik.

How about them nix?

#046 Tux's regret

N: Poor Tux, one night of wining and dining led to a lifetime of royalties up in smoke! S: It happens to the best of us.

What are your regrets usually a result of?

Overdrinking, ... *this also includes coffee and cola.* 9%

Oversleeping, ... *or are you an under sleeper?* 19%

Overeating, ... *if I'm not overeating here, I'm over eating at my mom's.* 14%

Overworking, ... *I used to over work, then I got over working by putting myself over working.* 15%

Being way too cool for my own good, ... *ah, it is the burden we super cool must carry in cool silence.* 29%

I viewed the results. *don't you regret not voting?* 11%

May not add up to exactly 100% due to rounding and regrets. I've had a few, but then again, too few to mention.

#201 Coming Out

N: Next week this family will be guest starring on Jerry Springer, and the son and father nearly come to blows, while the mother screams and cries hysterically, and the audience starts fighting!

What do you want to come out from?

My rock, ... *I recommend using sunscreen for the first few days.* 4%

My shell, ... *have you been hiding under your shell account again?* 11%

The shadow of another, ... *has your nick been particularly extroverted lately?* 4%

My geekosphere, ... *how long can a geek survive outside of one?* 10%

I've been looking for something to crawl under lately, ... *NitroKitty prefers blankets.* 36%

I viewed the results from my hiding place. 12%

May not add up to exactly 100% due to rounding and data coming out.

#162 Jeopardy

S: Jeopardy is the perfect game show for geeks, as they are particularly adept at "questioning" answers.

What would your answer have been?

What is the story of my life, ... *I'm sorry, but that's only the most fascinating topic of conversation of the 21st century.* 4%

What is the value of Pi, ... *now I know you're a math geek.* 15%

What was the better TV series, Gilligan's Island or I Dream of Jeannie, ... *does stranded with Ginger and Mary Anne compare with finding a Jeannie?* 19%

What is a geek, ... *almost as hard to pin down as that value of Pi.* 15%

Why is the Jeopardy sign two different colors, ... *isn't this also related to that Meaning of Life question?* 26%

Don't rush me, I'm still thinking about it. 18%

May not add up to exactly 100% due to rounding and the omnipotence of Alex Trebek.

#176 Alien Reinactment

S: This comic just reinforces those old stereotypes! N: What, about Linux programmers having long hair and beards? S: No, about aliens being obsessed with Earth culture! N: Here's a TV show idea: Apple Eye for the Linux Guy!

If you were attending Earth OS Fest, which Linux/GNU celebrity would you dress up as?

Linus Torvalds, ... *his AY2K Transmeta look is cool.* 7%

Jon "maddog" Hall, ... *his costume also requires a mammalian epidermis outgrowth.* 4%

Larry Wall, ... *his flamboyant style has real sex-a-perl.* 5%

Eric Raymond, ... *the "Geeks with Disintegrator Rays" side trip is always a blast at these conventions.* 2%

Richard Stallman, ... *"Free as in vocal utterances, not as in Soylent Green".* 3%

I look more like Tux, ... *are you sure you don't mean Homer Simpson?* 29%

I'd dress up as one of the other OS's celebrities, ... *the Steve Jobs turtle neck and sweater is amazingly comfy.* 35%

I'm working a booth. 12%

May not add up to exactly 100% due to rounding and the data weighing less in Alien comic worlds.

#477 The Sheriff

N: I wonder if Linus ever thinks he's created a monster or Pandora's box? S: Heh... what if Linus had never created Linux... all that geek energy would have been directed towards something else... like watching Star Trek!

Which movie cowboy is Linus Torvalds most like?

John Wayne, ... *he's got True Grit.* 4%

Roy Rogers, ... *that's sure to Trigger some memories.* 5%

Clint Eastwood, ... *go ahead, make my data.* 5%

Gary Cooper, ... *we're all waiting for High Noon in Redmond.* 5%

Jimmy Stewart, ... *the Man Who Shot Liberty Stallman?* 19%

A Leningrad Cowboy, ... *well, he did Go America.* 21%

Linus has traits of them all, ... *makes sense, he seems to incorporate little bits of everyone.* 16%

This is a protest vote for CowboyNeal. 22%

May not add up to exactly 100% due to rounding and the posse's round up.

#195 Hot Rodder

N: Maybe Stephen King will write a book called, "Christine II, the CPU," where a computer slowly but surely murders its users. S: I think Pogue is writing that, only it's called "Windows: the Missing Manual."

How do you like to accelerate your computer?

CPU upgrades, ... *remember when they removed Spock's brain?* 12%

Hard drive upgrades, ... *just what I need, more space to store my junk.* 3%

Ram upgrades, ... *no, I don't think you can upgrade a Dodge Ram.* 24%

I just buy a newer model, ... *if you can't fight Moore's Law, join it.* 17%

I throw it as hard as I can, ... *it almost guarantees you'll end up getting a new computer of some sort eventually.* 30%

I accelerated the voting process. 12%

May not add up to exactly 100% due to rounding and flame decals.

#082 Slashdot Karma

N: That would be the equivalent of coal in your Christmas stocking. S: Or maybe a rock in your halloween candy? (oh oh... there goes my karma!)

What unit of measurement is Slashdot karma measured in anyway?

Maiuabars, ... *a Maiua unit of pressure, equaling about one million flames. Such intense pressures usually originate deep inside the earth, in a place inhabited by trolls.* 5%

Hemospower, ... *a unit of work or energy equal to the work done at the rate of one Hemos for one hour. Note, this unit has been known to fluctuate wildly.* 5%

Cowboy Newtons, ... *a force of one Cowboy Newton will accelerate a mass of one fig newton at the rate of one meter per second per second cowboy.* 11%

TacoWatt, ... *a metric unit of power equal to one trillion (1012) Tacos or about 1.341 billion Hemospower (if Hemos has consumed one trillion tacos).* 22%

Timquency, *a unit of measurement equal to the number of stories being posted by Timothy at this very second. Not to be confused with the Timbit, a delicious Tim Horton's treat.* 2%

KiloKatz, ... *a common unit of work or energy, equaling the amount of energy consumed while replying to a Jon Katz story. Not to be confused with the Kill-a-Katz, a unit of measurement used to describe the intensity of mental illness in trolls.* 8%

Cupcakes, ... *a Slashdot cupcake is a unit used by cartoon scientists to describe an ethereal and transcendentally perfect Slashdot "moment." A related measurement, the nibble, is 4 bits or 1/2 big byte of such a cupcake.* 27%

I viewed the results, and now would like a cupcake please. 17%

May not add up to exactly 100% due to rounding and first posts.

#019 Legal advice

N: Ironically, it is Larry Ewing who doesn't see royalties from the widespread use of his Tux artwork. I wonder if that bugs him, or whether the spin offs and glory make up for it? S: I bet comics that feature Tux help too.

You can do the JoyPoll for this comic, ...exclusively for those who have this book! Find it online here...
http://www.joyoftech.com/joyoftech/thebestofjot/index.html

#052 Mac User's Triumph

N: This is a depiction of a true event that happened to Snaggy. The feeling of achievement afterwards was amazing. S: After you drew the depiction or after I mounted the floppy?

What was your early triumph on the computer?

Turning it on and off properly, ...*you mean you shouldn't just pull the plug?* 3%

Mastering the mouse, ... *my Repetitive Stress Injuries suggest the mouse has mastered me.* 2%

Figuring out where stuff got saved, ... *you mean you don't save to the CANCEL folder?* 13%

Hello World, ... *did you ever get an answer back?* 31%

Goodbye social life, ... *it didn't disappear, it was just digitized.* 36%

I triumphantly viewed the results! 12%

May not add up to exactly 100% due to rounding and repetitive rounding injuries.

#065 Unix Genes

N: Well, the good news is she has a free babysitter, the computer! S: That's the bad news too!

What is your dominant gene?

The Work/Eat/Sleep Gene, ... *sometimes called the 20th Century gene.* 16%

The Gamer Gene, ... *your actions are ruled by your joystick.* 10%

The Roddenberry Gene, ... *it drives you to go where no man has gone before.* 13%

The Slacker Gene, ... *its influence is often masked by a dominant work gene, however it is always passed on to future generations.* 24%

Every gene I have is recessive, ... *you're a good candidate for assimilation.* 24%

I'm viewing the results from inside a double helix. 9%

May not add up to exactly 100% due to rounding and sugar, phosphate, cytosine, guanine, adenine and thymine.

#024 Phonetics Investigator

S: What an exciting TV show Betty the Phonetics Investigator would be! Set in libraries across the country, with Betty solving grammer and pronunciation crimes... with only the Dewey Decimal System for backup! CSI for nerds!

How do you pronounce Linux?

Just like my grandpappy did. 9%

In Swedish, with a Finnish accent. 25%

With my mouth full, usually. 15%

I prefer the original Klingon. 48%

Will almost positively not add up to exactly 100% due to rounding, often.

#338 Linux Guru in a Can

N: How can you tell if the Guru's gone bad in that can? S: You cannot. Besides, it makes little difference to how he smells after you open it.

What kind of instant tech support do you need?

Linux Guru in a can, ... *even more satisfying when served with a side order of Instant Mashed Windows.* 2%

Mac Genius power bar, ... *packed with 10 essential Cease and Desists!* 4%

Windows Wizard tablets, ... *take the whole bottle, and still have a headache in the morning.* 1%

Instant Techno Talking Babe, ... *they're fine at first, but after a year or so can turn into Techno-Nagging Bitches. ;)* 53%

I don't need it, I give it, ... *that must be instantly gratifying.* 29%

I popped the results. 9%

May not add up to exactly 100% due to rounding and not enough MSG.

#240 Linux Lass part 1

S: Nitrozac once went with me to a meeting of amateur astronomers... I was lucky the collective hopes and dreams of all the telescope geeks didn't turn her into Newtonian Girl!

So what exactly is a warp optimization rift?

It's like a cloud thingy that's all warped and optimized, ... *in other words, silent but deadly.* 8%

It's a fight between the Warps and the Optimizations, ... *isn't that the plot of the new Star Trek series?* 2%

It's a bug in the Linux kernel, ... *it's not a bug, it's a feature!* 10%

It's the non-proprietary way Open Source geeks create their superheroes, ... *but isn't Apple's iHero so much easier to use?* 43%

It's the thing I've been stuck in lately, ... *blame it on the space-time weather.* 21%

I'm viewing the warped results. 13%

May not add up to exactly 100% due to rounding and the collective hopes and dreams of other JoyPollers.

#241 Linux Lass part 2

N: Don't you just hate it when "the man" shows up at the library! S: I don't mind really, especially if I get a good view of the librarians tearing off their clothes between the bookshelves.

What's your favorite SatanSoft product?

SatanSoft ME ME ME edition, ... *it's more like a THEM THEM THEM edition.* 3%

SatanSoft Office of Doom, ... *includes Satan's Word, Excel Hell, Dante's Outlook, and PowerPoint of No Return.* 4%

Satan's Entourage, ... *it sends you lots of hotmail.* 4%

The Blue Screensaver of Death, ... *it runs every 10 minutes or so despite your settings.* 19%

I'm still kinda watching Lynn Nicks change between the bookshelves, ... *she's the patron saint of Software Salvation.* 52%

My SatanSoft browser didn't want me to vote. 15%

May not add up to exactly 100% due to rounding and your secret identity.

#251 Linux Lass part 3

N: Now, that's a super power—the ability to decypher legalese! S: I thought her super power was that awesome awe-inspiring alliteration!

In your humble opinion, what is Linux Lass's greatest power?

Her power of Open Source, ... *open, as in beer?* 6%

Her intimate knowledge of legalese, ... *it's rumored she dated a law student in college.* 5%

Her ability to rip licenses in half, ... *we're talking 20-pound bond paper!* 11%

Her ability to strike back at evildoers with name-calling like "fuzzbald" and "proprietary pimp," ... *evildoers just hate being teased.* 16%

Her impeccable sense of super heroine fashion, ... *well, according to the union rules, it's gotta be eye-catching and comfortable, easily changeable within seconds, and skin tight.* 46%

I think her real power is that she's a librarian. 13%

May not add up to exactly 100% due to rounding and card catalog collapse.

Joy of Mac

#223 X-Specs

N: Ironically, X-Ray specs reveal more about the wearer than the person X-ray spec'd.

What Specs do you usually wear?

X Specs, ... *watch out for all that Carbon on the lenses.* 12%

Classic MacOS Specs, ... *they're great, except for that unprotected magnification.* 15%

Penguin-powered Shades, ... *you always did look good with a Tux.* 17%

Windows Blinders, ... *they block out all that distracting competition.* 7%

Sun Goggles, ... *do you see a bright future?* 5%

I wear dual-boot focals, ... *have you tried chip-ons?* 20%

When it comes to computer vision, I'm blind, ... *sometimes it's better not to know you're about to crash.* 6%

I viewed the results, but just barely. 13%

May not add up to exactly 100% due to rounding and astigmatism.

#309 User Group Family

N: Soon we'll be seeing MUG family counselling for dysfunctional MUG families. "If Grandma asks about AppleWorks one more time, I'm gonna...."
S: Fan Brent wrote in with this fun tidbit.... "I liked the Joy of Tech episode where the guy takes his girlfriend to a Mac User Group meeting telling her that he was taking her to his family. I kind of did something like that a few years back with my fiance when I told her I was taking her to my favorite vacation spot which happened to be MacWorld Expo NYC! We had a great time at MacWorld and got to see the ever cool G4 Cube. She asked me if it was a toaster!"

If you were at this meeting, which cluster of geeks would you gravitate to?

I'd go welcome the boyfriend and his newbie girlfriend, ... *then ask her what her intentions are.* 7%

The group of guys talking about the iPod, ... *ya, tonight they're passing out copies of Office.* 8%

One guy, two girls, and that Missing Manual, ... *isn't that the title of a French movie?* 37%

The two hacker kids who look like they're getting into trouble, ... *they're not getting into trouble, they are just installing one of those copies of Office.* 10%

The guy in the back typing away to himself, ... *he's programming the meeting to self-destruct in three hours.* 5%

If you were at this meeting, which cluster of geeks would you gravitate to? *(continued)*

I'd find a corner and hide, ... *at this meeting, you can run Office, but you can't hide.* 15%

I'm viewing the results, and will be giving a presentation on them. 14%

May not add up to exactly 100% due to rounding and someone raffling off a few percentage points.

#378 Walter's Grip

N: I love the stories of Newton enthusiasts holding up their Newtons in silent protest at Steve Jobs's keynotes. S: Do you think Steve ever goes to Newton User Group meetings and holds up an iPod?

So how do you think Walter died?

He was discontinued by his maker, ... *and now he clutches his Newton in silent protest.* 22%

He died of excitement, ... *I guess that Woz rumor was too much for his wheels.* 2%

He was part of a suicide cult of Mac, ... *they died from shooting themselves in the foot.* 12%

He was hit in the head by an Apple, ... *somebody made the mistake of tossing him his MessagePad.* 7%

Newton geeks don't die. He'll come back, I know he will, ... *the handwriting recognition is on the wall!* 41%

His PDA was DOA. 13%

May not add up to exactly 100% due to rounding and the Stylus Council.

#103 Temple of Worship

N: MacWorld Expo, a place to renew your faith in Jobs, share fellowship with other Mac Heads, and pray for cool, new hardware. S: And for those who can't make it... weep at the wailing wall.

What sacred OS place do you worship at?

The Mac Temple, ... *have you read the Book of Jobs?* 22%

The Altar of Be, ... *an internet appliance is a very devoted device.* 2%

The Chapel of Linux, ... *The Gospel of the Norse God.* 18%

The Church of BSD, ... *you wouldn't happen to one of those Unix Eunuchs would you?* 3%

I worship at some other OS shrine, ... *in the end, we all pay tribute to the same Spirits of Silicon.* 3%

I spend most of my time in Windows Hell, ... *you'll never find yourself at the Perl-ie Gates.* 18%

My desk. I'm a Geek God, ... *a figment of geek mythology perhaps. ;-)* 20%

What sacred OS place do you worship at? *(continued)*

My desk. I'm a Geek God, ... *a figment of geek mythology perhaps. ;-)* 20%

I agnostically viewed the results. 10%

May not add up to exactly 100% due to rounding and OS Existentialism.

#104 Sex in the City

S: When the TiBook showed up at the party, a lot of geeks fell hopelessly in love. DigitalBill describes his love affair... "Ti was the laptop that finally ended my relationship with desktop computing, ... oh, she was thin and gorgeous, sure, but soooo powerful... and you KNOW how sexy power is..."

What is the sexiest thing about the new G4 PowerBook?

All that sexy software bundled up with it, ... *I bet it would look especially sexy bundled up in a T-igloo.* Less than 1%

The titillating Titanium, ... *it has you all a titter, doesn't it?* 21%

It is certified to run OS X, ... *I can't wait for OS XXX!* 12%

Its very slim profile, ... *it's nicknamed the super-waif model.* 4%

More power = sexier, ... *Bill Gates is an exception to that rule. ;-)* 10%

How unattainable one is, ... *in this case, I doubt the passion would burn out.* 12%

I'm sorry, but I just not super turned on, ... *oh well, geek to his own I suppose.* 28%

I viewed the results, with just a bit a drool. 14%

May not add up to exactly 100% due to rounding and interference from a reality distortion field.

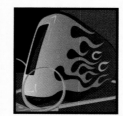

#136 HotWheels iMac

N: How cool would this computer be? MacAddict Magazine selected my design in an iMac mod contest a while back. Cool!

What's your favorite hot thing?

Hot Wheels, ... *I had the standard Hot Wheels loop the loop, plus SIZZLERS with the Power Pit! What did you have?* 7%

Hot rods, ... *I guess many of you would rather work on hot mods.* 3%

Hot dogs, ... *especially yummy during those dog days.* 8%

Hot pants, ... *as seen on AfterY2K!* 53%

All of the above, and in that order, ... *and on the same day? Whoa!* 16%

I viewed the results, or perhaps liked them in a different order. 10%

May not add up to exactly 100% due to rounding and the Evil Weevil.

#243 The Megahertz Myth part 1

S: Apple went to great lengths to explain to people why their G4 chips were just as fast or faster than Intel chips of higher frequency... they called it the "megahertz myth." After Nitrozac fell into a coma while listening to Jon Rubenstein's keynote explanation of chip architecture, we decided to spice up the myth, and turn it into a storybook. At the very least, we though it would make good bedtime reading.

Aside from temperature, who's hotter?

The Pentium 4, ... *be careful, or you'll get a clock throttling!* 3%

The SPARC III, ... *it's gotta be hot if there's a Sun involved.* 9%

The Itanium, ... *do you think they really wanted to call it Titanium?* 4%

The G4, ... *you must mean the PowerPC MPC7410 (code named "Nitro"). ;)* 40%

I'm more of a RAM man, ... *chips may come and go, but RAM has legs.* 21%

I'm humming that darn Intel four note theme song. 19%

May not add up to exactly 100% due to rounding and heat sinking.

#244 The Megahertz Myth part 2

N: Jon's groovy shirt is inspired by the original Apple logo colors. S: I like the Techie Godfather sparkles!

Who are your least favorite inhabitants of the Land of Tech?

The Marketing Fairies, ... *but their little office dances are so incredible, ... so robust!* 18%

The Vulture Capitalists, ... *but if it wasn't for them, who would pick clean the bones?* 8%

The GNU Gnomes, ... *not all of them are diminutive, deformed humans who live underground.* 3%

The Pirates of Proprietarianism, ... *but aren't they the ones who built the Land of Tech?* 22%

The Loser Usrs, ... *most of them are gentle folk, they wouldn't harm the coffee cup holder on their computer.* 10%

The Trolls, ... *but they power the page view economy.* 14%

Every ecosystem needs scavengers, even the Land of Tech, ... *I thought that's what the cartoonists were for.* 9%

I'm voting for myself. 11%

May not add up to exactly 100% due to rounding and the Lord of the Pings.

#245 The Megahertz Myth part 3

N: The G4 is really mimicking the audience at Jon's keynote presentation. S: Um, Nitro, you forget that most of the audience are geeks... I was riveted by all the techno-babble and on the edge of my Quicktime-streaming seat!

What is the G4 really doing in the second panel?

The classic eyes-glazing-over, ... *I get it when eyeing glazed donuts.* 16%

The classic boredom-induced-brain-bleeding, ... *or did he get a bit too much information?* 19%

Wondering if he left the stove on, ... *he just hates to overheat.* 11%

Planning his escape route, ... *his only hope is via a cpu upgrade ... yeah right.. as zif!* 26%

Trying to make the moment last forever, ... *it won't, not with a velocity engine involved.* 13%

My pipeline just flushed. 13%

May not add up to exactly 100% due to rounding and insertion force equaling zero.

#246 The Megahertz Myth part 4

S: This has got to be one of my favorite scenes in a Joy of Tech... the pie processing contest. N: Eating pie, I knew that would get your attention!

What charges your capacitor?

Pie! Apple, cherry, pumpkin...YUM, ... *oh, for a brief moment there I though you meant Pi.* 9%

A good strong brew, ... *are you talking CH 3CH 2OH, or C 8H10N 4O2?* 14%

My Significant Other, ... *what do you use as a dielectric?* 21%

Websites that feature photographic representations of Potentially Significant Others, ... *you've been drooling over hardware sites again, haven't you?* 23%

Technology myths illustrated in storybook format, ... *keep on geek'in, and one day you may be part of the mythology. ;)* 19%

I'm resistoring voting. 11%

May not add up to exactly 100% due to rounding and the number of farads that can dance on the head of a pin.

#247 The Megahertz Myth part 5

N: Hey, the Techie Godfather forgot to say "bibbledeebobbledyboo!" S: He didn't want to reveal his password!

What kind of carriage would you take to the Expo?

A crystal Apple logo carriage would work for me, ... *after midnight, it turns into a Lisa.* 19%

I'd proudly take the Open Source van, ... *just watch out for all those backseat drivers.* 14%

I'm already on the Microsoft SatanSled, ... *heh, it's an express, straight to Window's Hell.* 6%

I'm waiting for an old AmigaMobile, ... *don't wait too long, or you'll miss the whole Expo.* 7%

I'm hoping for a Nitrozac-drawn carriage, ... *you never know, perhaps she'll pencil you in.* 39%

My vote turned into a pumpkin. 11%

May not add up to exactly 100% due to rounding and three ugly step-datas.

#248 The Megahertz Myth part 6

N: That's a good look for Jobs I think, the crown and stuff. S: You're just sucking up to the Prince of Expos!

What is your Royal Title?

Princess Slackinov, ... *is that what all that Free Slackinov stuff is about?* 14%

Duke of Perl, ... *Duke, Duke, Duke, Duke of Perl, Duke, Duke, Duke of Perl, Duke, Duke, Duke of Perl, Duke, Duke, Duke of URL...* 18%

Sir PhotoShop, ... *do you use the knight-vision filter?* 6%

King of HTML, ... *ruler of a fractured kingdom with many standards.* 7%

The Court Macster, ... *will you sing an iTune for free?* 23%

Queen Bitch, ... *well that's just Hunky Dory, ... do you wear a frock coat and bipperty-bopperty hat? :)* 9%

I serfed my way here. 21%

May not add up to exactly 100% due to rounding and the Magna Carta.

#249 The Megahertz Myth part 7

N: Wait till G5 comes and beats up his little brother and takes his place! S: * sigh * I feel like Snaggy-rella, left behind at the G5 Ball.

What is the moral of this story?

Steve Jobs has a wonderful singing voice, ... *coming soon to an iPod near you!* 6%

Microchips are petty little things, ... *well, apparently the expo circuit is just brutal.* 3%

Size isn't everything, especially if you're an ugly duckling, freakishly-Rudolphian Cinderella type, ... *watch out, you'll end up at the Expo of Misfit Toys.* 12%

Sometimes it takes a myth to make people feel a little bit better, ... *and upgrade a little faster.* 12%

Somebody slipped something into Snaggy's Kool-aid, ... *Bad Simon! Bad teddy bear!* 50%

I viewed the morels. 13%

May not add up to exactly 100% due to rounding and Yukon Cornelius.

#207 The Ides of MacWorld

N: I guess the Sphere didn't make the cut, it probably did a Romeo and Juliet and rolled off the desk. S: The Sphere DID make the cut... they cut it in half and used it as the new iMac base!

What Ides do you tend to beware of?

The Ides of MacWorld Expo, ... *which no doubt will result in a lot of drool.* 3%

The Ides of Discontinued Hardware, ... *I come not to praise old hardware, just use it.* 7%

The Ides of Microsoft, ... *they stab it with their steely knives but they just can't kill the beast.* 40%

The Ides of Snaggy, ... *but nothing compared to the Ides of NitroKitty.* 2%

The Ides a b'y that builds the boat, ... *beware of geeks building ships.* 6%

I tend to beware of Soothsayers, ... *cartoonists sometimes suffer the same fate.* 25%

I felt the comic was too Brutus. 14%

May not add up to exactly 100% due to rounding and friends, Romans and countrymen.

#217 Planet of the X

N: There must be more gravity on Planet of the X, ... that would account for the heavy, sluggish performance.

What OS World are you stranded on?

The Planet of the X, ... *no, Planet of the XXX wass not an option.* 8%

Windows World, ... *Bill's World, Bill's World, Party time, Excellent!* 16%

The Land of the Linux, ... *aren't Penguins the dominant form of life there?* 12%

Mac OS 9 from Outer Space, ... *also known as It Came from Cupertino!* 12%

It's not a planet, it's a Sun OS, ... *that's right, everything revolves around you, doesn't it.* 3%

The Forbidden OS, ... *it's only a monster of your imagination.* 7%

I'm not stranded, I willingly live here, ... *that's what all castaways say after a while.* 24%

I observed the results. 13%

May not add up to exactly 100% due to rounding and the data-roid belts.

#333 Nightmare in Cupertino

S: Nine is Fine and in my humble experience, a lot faster, but I can't live without iChat and Safari. N: Nine's Alive! It's Alive! S: I love Steve's blanket... which gets its inspiration from the old Mac OS teddy bear clipboard.

What's the scariest part of Steve Jobs's nightmare?

The rotting corpse of OS 9, rebooting from its grave, ... *does it seek flesh, or RAM?* 7%

The mob of crazed mac-zombies, ... *they're not mac-zombies... THEY'RE DEVELOPERS, DEVELOPERS, DEVELOPERS!!!* 11%

The fact that it suggests Steve Jobs does indeed sleep, ... *maybe it's a nap-mare?* 19%

That teddy bear blanket, ... *he should have slept with David Pogue's bear!* 19%

It's not a nightmare... it's actually happening! ... *"get out of the house... it's coming from your Mac!"* 19%

The scariest part is that there's no popcorn sold during the comic. 15%

May not add up to exactly 100% due to rounding and undead undoes.

#255 iMovie

S: After this comic appeared, Nitro and I received an email from Apple's iMovie developers... they liked it!

What's taking all your time lately?

What's taking all your time lately?

My obsession to document my life, ... *let's get digital, digital.* 2%

The documentation of other lives, ... *been watching the cam lately?* 2%

A big pile of documents, ... *been spending a lot of time in the old growth piles of paper?* 19%

I've been writing a lot of documentation, ... *doing any data doodling?* 11%

I've been watching a lot of documentaries, ... *been watching lots of "The making of..."?* 5%

My obsession to avoid my life, ... *would that include partaking in polls?* 45%

I'm still reading the poll documentation. 12%

May not add up to exactly 100% due to rounding and documentals.

#293 The Size of Music

N: What I would give to have so much living space that you can have a whole room dedicated to an obscure hobby!

Of the artists and bands recognizable in Dad's collection, which one do you like the most?

David Bowie, ... *a lad insane?* 11%

Elvis Costello, ... *his aim is true.* 12%

The Beatles, ... *ya ya ya!* 25%

KISS, ... *is that where "keep it simple stupid" comes from?* 5%

I've got that iPod commercial in my head, ... *ok, now let's see you do the dance.* 8%

I'm pretty sure there's some Kraftwerk in there somewhere, ... *and now you're the operator with your pocket calculator.* 20%

This is a protest vote in support of Twisted Sister, the Human League, and the Geek Culture Club. 16%

May not add up to exactly 100% due to rounding and .-. -
-.. .. ... .-.-.- ... ..- -. -...

#185 A Genius Question

N: The hardest part of being a Mac Genius would be resisting the urge to pick up the red phone and ask if their fridge is running.

What's the moral of this cartoon?

Never use the red phone, ... *it's only for Genius Emergencies.* 16%

Always wear an undershirt, ... *clean underwear helps too.* 13%

Asking a stupid question can make you a genius, ... *maybe they could hire a Magic 8 Ball.* 17%

When Life gives you lemons, make Applesauce, ... *and if your computer's a lemon, try Genius-aide.* 7%

We of this reality find cartoon suffering funny, ... *be careful what you laugh at, someday you may find yourself pixelated.* 25%

I'm phoning about the results. 18%

May not add up to exactly 100% due to rounding and staff turnover.

#307 Broom Genius

S: The Broom Genius rocks, I imagine this character to be the "Boothby" of the Apple Store. N: He's also the lightbulb genius and the children's-section-upchuck-removal engineer.

What kind of Genius are you?

Broom Genius, ... *this has nothing to do with witches or Wizards does it?* 1%

Garbage Genius, ... *I'm no genius, but I know it when I see it.* 1%

Computer Genius, ... *now is that a load of garbage, or an oxymoron?* 9%

Mac Genius, ... *not an oxymoron, it's a double affirmation!* 18%

Lord of the Geniuses, ... *one brain to rule them all!* 11%

I'm smart enough to know I'm no Genius, ... *"The fool thinks himself to be wise, but the wise man knows himself to be a fool." - ancient Klingon saying.* 46%

I'm viewing the results of geniuses. 11%

May not add up to exactly 100% due to rounding and someone Mensa-ing with the data.

#337 extensions

N: Wouldn't you know it, there really is a blonde genius working at an Apple Store that looks shockingly similar to this girl. Is that the sound of thousands of sneakered feet running to the Apple store?

What happened next?

The blonde genius, in a very professional manner, rebooted his TiBook without extensions, ... *now there's a shift! What a Classic blonde.* 8%

The blonde genius was fired for being rude to slimy customers, ... *she tried to fight it in court, but alas Apple hired the Legal Geniuses.* 1%

The man apologized for being kind of a jerk, then they kissed and made up, ... *um, ya, right... I think your pram needs zapping.* 7%

A male genius walked up and said "I know what is wrong," then pushed her out of the way, ... *they were dating, now he's her X.* 6%

The customer made a moronic reply, and he's now using a eunuch's operating system, ... *wow, that chick has balls!* 58%

I'm gonna click back and view the blonde genius again. 16%

May not add up to exactly 100% due to rounding and prime numbers having more fun.

#350 Apple Store Wedding

N: But the big question is... What offspring would they produce? A Unix Guru? S: I think the real question is will they stay together long enough to have kids?

What would be your ideal wedding?

Married by Woz, honeymoon in Cupertino, ... *that's sounds better than Jobs's Nightmare in Cupertino.* 14%

Married by Linus, honeymoon inside a giant papier-mache Tux, ... *wow, do you think Martha Stewart will do the catering?* 3%

Married by Captain Picard, honeymoon on Risa, ... *can Wil Wheaton be the ring bearer?* 27%

Married by Nitrozac, honeymoon in the Cartoon Universe, ... *cool, do ya think it would be like one of her medal ceremonies?* 26%

Married by noon, separated by midnight, ... *and perhaps reconciled by dawn.* 8%

Always a JoyPollmaid, never a JoyPollvoter? 19%

May not add up to exactly 100% due to rounding and the reception party.

#192 If Microsoft had a Genius Bar

S: We thought it'd be fun to imagine a Microsoft version of Apple's Genius Bar. The Brainiac Bar logo is an adaptation of the electrodes on Brainiac's head (Superman's arch rival). N: Hmmm, would Lex Luther have an Evil Genius Bar?

What would be the worst thing about a Microsoft Store?

It would be a place to find all of Microsoft's products under one roof, ... *shopping can be Hell.* 27%

Its storefront would be nothing but Windows, ... *what's that old saying about not letting a gnu run loose in a windows shop?* 11%

It would end up monopolizing the whole mall, ... *it's not monopolizing, it's shopping innovation.* 35%

I would probably end up working there, ... *selling one's soul to the company store is a time honored tradition.* 5%

I'd shop 'til I drop, ... *you're more likely to crash.* 1%

I'd pay not to shop there. 17%

May not add up to exactly 100% due to rounding and constantly picking on Bill.

#188 Genius VS Genius

N: This is our spoof of those hilarious Mad Magazine cartoons, Spy VS Spy. Somehow it's funny to think that there's rivalry, scheming, and pranks going on amongst the Mac Genuises. S: Not so funny if you've just dropped off your computer for repairs!

In a Genius vs. Genius Arms Race, what is the greatest weapon?

Fully caffeinated neurons, ... *you can only hide behind a defense shield of Jolt Cola for so long.* 17%

A well-stocked arsenal of t-shirts, ... *remember, not doing laundry can result in Mutually Assured Destruction.* 11%

The ability to Think Different, ... *especially if your nemesis starts lobbing Evian water bottles at you.* 23%

The Complete Works of David Pogue, ... *is that why they call it Camp David?* 9%

Real Geniuses are pacifists, ... *knowledge is the best deterrent.* 24%

I just ordered we go to DEFCON 1. 13%

May not add up to exactly 100% due to rounding and the Joke and Dagger Dept.

FEEL ANY DIFFERENT?

NOT REALLY. I ENDED UP GIVING HER MY EMAIL INSTEAD

#194 Genius VS Genius v.2

N: Bottled water is fine and all, but if only they served lovely sandwiches with the crusts cut off! S: All you can eat Genius Bar!

What would be the most ironic way to die in an Apple Store?

Of thirst at the Genius Bar, ... *all that Evian, but not a drop to drink.* 3%

Crashing through Windows, ... *or falling through a blue screen of death?* 58%

Slipping and falling on an iceBook, ... *the specs will knock you over too.* 5%

Over-drooling at the TiBooks, ... *keep an eye out for the Slippery with Drool signs.* 5%

Of an acute case of Geek Glee, ... *it starts with a Joy of Tech fever.* 9%

I exhumed the results. 16%

May not add up to exactly 100% due to rounding and dying on the Jobs.

Microsoft

#200 No Angel

S: A lot of geeks think Bill Gates is the personification of the Devil... but he must have another side to him, don't you think? Don't you? Hello? (Snaggy's question echos out into infinity...)

What little creatures do you have guiding your life?

Two devils, ... *luckily, the two tend to cancel each other out.* 8%

An angel and a devil, ... *are you sure you don't mean a coffee and a donut?* 9%

Nothing but the sweetest of angels, ... *we're talking about a lot of donuts here, aren't we.* 9%

My significant other, ... *who no doubt can be both angel and devil.* 13%

My kids, ... *how sweet, do your computers have names? ;)* 4%

My cat, ... *NitroKitty has been guiding our trip. ;)* 18%

My ISP, ... *ahhh, the giant devil!* 22%

I guide my own life, at least that's what my cat tells me. 13%

May not add up to exactly 100% due to rounding and little geek angels fighting over how to do the rounding.

#308 Klingon Pain Rituals

N: This is my personal favorite comic. It never fails to make me laugh no matter how many times I've seen it. I love the guys in the background in severe pain, and you know that it's gonna hurt even more to install that OS! The older Klingon seems to be guiding the young Klingons in their painful journey, and he's like older people who are skeptical of computers but still curious. Soon he'll be convinced that installing a Microsoft OS, will indeed be more painful than the pain stick. *chuckle*.

What is your pain ritual?

Getting up in the morning, ... *it's a daily ritual, hopefully.* 21%

Getting to work, ... *then having to return, that's "back pain?"* 8%

Meetings, ... *is this what is known as Pain Management?* 7%

Daytime TV, ... *but aren't strong painkillers called Oprah-oids?* 3%

Certain previously-named operating systems, ... *has your pain threshold be recently upgraded?* 16%

My life is more of a Pain Festival, ... *is that what the IRS is calling it now?* 17%

The word pain does not accurately reflect the agony of tech support, ... *and it's chronic!* 16%

Voting is a pain, just gimme the results! 9%

May not add up to exactly 100% due to rounding and pain being nothing to Tribble-ize.

#057 Monkeying around at Microsoft

S: Of course this comic does not apply to the fine monkeys over at Microsoft's Macintosh Business Unit. N: Do they work for Apples?

If you had an infinite number of monkeys, what would you get them to do?

Type, type, type!!!, ... *yep, they would eventually write the Complete Works of SPAM.* 15%

Design and build spaceships, ... *their past history in the space program should come in handy.* 24%

Take a toilet training course, ... *obviously, you have monkey experience.* 15%

Breed, so that I could have even more monkeys, ... *apparently, you can never have enough infinite monkeys.* 15%

Cut each other's paws off, so that I could have an infinite amount of wishes, ... *your first wish.... please get the knives away from those wounded monkeys!* 15%

I monkeyed around with the results. 14%

May not add up to exactly 100% due to rounding and the differences between King Kong and Mighty Joe Young.

#203 Despicability Field

S: This comic was inspired by the antitrust trials, but also by the intense hatred that Bill Gates seems to generate all on his own. If Steve Jobs has his Reality Distortion field... what would Bill have? The Alfred E. Newman-izing of Gates is inspired by an image Nitro originally made up in the primordial years of geekculture.com

What do you want to appeal today?™

The Court of Appeal's decision, ... *well, it wasn't meant to appeal to you, I guess.* 24%

I'd like to appeal my lack of sex appeal, ... *Bill Gates had the same problem, then he switched to loafers. LOL* 21%

I'd like to appeal the improper conduct of certain cartoonists towards Bill Gates, ... *let those without despicable cartoon thoughts cast the first pixel.* 5%

The leaky and toxic nature of Bill's Despicability Amplification Field, ... *it can even flow through Windows.* 20%

The way Nitrozac and Snaggy spell "Despicability", ... *we appeal to the mercy of the court... we haven't unpacked the dictionary yet.* 12%

I despise voting. 14%

May not add up to exactly 100% due to rounding and those who are rooting for the big guy.

#172 The Bug Zoo

S: There is a bug zoo in Victoria B.C. that two of our fans (Weirdarms and ARJ) visited. They posted in our Forums about their adventure, and that inspired this punny comic. N: If computer bugs eventually became rare, would Redmond be declared a National Bug Preserve?

What's your favorite Microsoft bug?

The paperclip that refuses to die, ... *he bugs a lot of people.* 11%

Their OS, ... *amazing how much money you can make selling bugs.* 40%

The Billipede, ... *apparently unsquashable.* 6%

It's not a bug, it's a feature, ... *ya, the little bomb or the blue screen means it's time to stretch your legs.* 33%

I'm bugged by the results. 8%

May not add up to exactly 100% due to rounding and arthropods.

#271 Stress Relief Dart Board

S: After the wrist slapping Microsoft received at the conclusion of the DOJ monopoly trial, we thought people might need to blow off a little steam. Bill is often the target of verbal insults, so this image came naturally, and it was a popular selling poster in our webstore. (In the interest of the book's safety though, we recommend using only Nerf weapons or mind darts.)

What kind of stress relief works for you?

Darts help,... *all that exercise is good for geeks.* 5%

Voodoo dolls,... *hmmm, do your friends needle you about that?* 10%

D e e p belly breaths,... *on your mark, get set,.... breathe!* 3%

Nothing works! Never! Ever,... *not even a good rant?* 16%

I try to get away from it all,... *that's what wireless was invented for. ;)* 10%

Comics!,... *neat! We're feeling a bit calmer over here now too.* 43%

I'm about to go bowling. 9%

May not add up to exactly 100% due to rounding and some old dart.

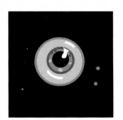

#116 The DNS Zone

S: Inspired by a Microsoft DNS outage that left their website MIA for a couple of days. Don't sweat it MS, it can happen to the best of us.   It would be cool though if every time your website went offline, Rod Serling would show up to break the news to you.

What Zone have you found yourself in lately?

No Parking Zone,... *no parking zones are a denial of service.* 8%

The End Zone,... *well, if you can make it through 'til Sunday night, you might be a SuperBowl Survivor.* 4%

The Phantom Zone,... *was this for hacking into Kryptonian servers?* 9%

The Zone of Geeking Out,... *it's when time stands still around your geek-o-sphere.* 15%

I'm zoned out,... *are you sure you're not just zonked, zapped, or zombie-like?* 51%

I viewed the results from the Twilight Zone. 9%

May not add up to exactly 100% due to rounding and time zones.

#294 Future Man

N: It's the happy man from the future! For his sake, I hope his time machine isn't running Windows.   S: And hopefully his Software Update won't kick in while he's back here, and re-install all the old versions of his aps.

What would you do with Mr. Future?

Club him, and take his tech,... *as any primitive geek would do.* 26%

Tell him to go back further into the past and change that future,... *have him open a little saving's account while he's at it too.* 31%

Kidnap him, and force him to sell stuff at your next Expo booth, ... *cash in on the electric tie craze before it happens!* 3%

Tell him to please turn down his electric tie,... *it's confusing traffic!* 5%

Slap him silly, since he called you a primitive geek,... *are you sure it wasn't a compliment?* 18%

Worship the guy, Ewok style, ... *and be thankful the 70's aren't back in style in the year 3000.* 3%

I viewed the results,... *tomorrow.* 12%

May not add up to exactly 100% due to rounding and history being written by that Victor fellow.

AY2K #333 A Tempting Offer.

S: Our comic, After Y2K, was a cult hit, but we were having trouble moving into print work, as new readers (and publishers) found it difficult to jump into its complicated storyline and characters. This comic, although officially an AY2K episode, was actually a test of a new format, a somewhat simpler comic, more timely, that almost anyone could get without too much background. The amount of positive feedback we received over this episode and other tests (like AY2K #328, The Break-up Game) confirmed to us that the decision to start a new comic (The Joy of Tech) would be a good one.

N: ZorroTheFox, one of our most colorful Forum members, is very fond of the SatanSoft Girl. I think he's already given his soul to her.

What do you think Satansoft makes?

Red hot chili pepper toilet paper,... *say that 4 times fast.* 10%

Proprietary something or other,... *hell is full of cool stuff that nobody gets to play with!* 27%

Any kind of program that runs on Windows,... *is it the programs, or the OS that is hell on earth?* 30%

It's actually pronounced Sat n' Soft, and they make saturated fat that softens your skin,... *it works from the inside out.* 9%

I viewed the results,... *it's rather refreshing!* 22%

May not add up to exactly 100% due to rounding and other hellish punishments.

#450 Microsoft Migration Kit

S: After Apple brought out it's highly visible and successful Switcher campaign, Microsoft struck back with it own "innovative" attempt. We couldn't resist putting together a virtual MS Kit of our own. We offered the button on our store as a lark... surprisingly it's been a popular add-on to orders. I guess we do have a lot of Windows shoppers!

What would be your main reason to migrate to Windows?

I'm into self-abuse, ... *no pain, no gain?* 18%

A Switcher double dared me, ... *what are you, a man, or a two-button mouse?* 2%

I have an extra computer, and need a good laugh, ... *it's not nice getting your kicks torturing computers like that.* 28%

Hmmm, body snatchers, ... *did it start with those Windows iPods?* 15%

I've already migrated, and boy, are my arms tired, ... *probably not as tired as your cold dead hands.* 4%

I'm already a native citizen of Windows, ... *maybe you could immigrate?* 11%

I bought a View-the Results Kit 19%

May not add up to exactly 100% due to rounding and not wanting to feel left out when everyone else is jumping off a cliff.

#259 Billy Gates

S: We love doing parody movie posters... I think part of the fun is imagining what the movie would actually be like. N: You know he wouldn't be wearing that sharp little wizard outfit, he'd insist on a frumpy wizard sweater.

So what do you think is Billy Gates' most impressive wizard power?

His Spell of Acquisition, ... *in the time it takes to read this, he may have bought you.* 7%

His ability to conjure up other people's good ideas, ... *I bet he got that idea from somewhere.* 46%

His Antitrust Incantations, ... *all those hours spend sticking pins in the Janet Reno voodoo doll seem to have paid off.* 15%

His psychokenetic abilities. For instance, animating a paperclip with his mind, ... *poor Clippy, the rest of us just want to un-animate him.* 6%

The patience to stay with Lord Ballmer all these years, ... *they are stuck with each other, it was part of that deal with the Devil.* 13%

I cursed the results. 10%

May not add up to exactly 100% due to rounding, and the Goblet of Gob.

SCI FI section

#111 The Dot Com Excavation

S: A few years ago, the video game Asteroids almost caused the extinction of my bank account! N: Hyperspace! Hyperspace!!!

In the year 2525, will geeks still be alive?

Nope, ... *heh, isn't that what they said 524 years ago?* Less than 1%

Yes, ... *great, cause I'm hoping someone will help me install Mac OS DXXXIV.* 19%

There will be geeks, but just not in the form we know them today, ... *they are still called geeks, but are more commonly known as Soylent Geek.* 48%

Oh god, I hope not, ... *as the apes in the year 2525 like to say, Get your hands off me, you stinking geek!* 4%

I'd just want to point out that the year 2525 is not a Millennial year, ... *not millennial, but kinda symetrical!* 18%

I survived the results. 8%

May not add up to exactly 100% due to rounding and Zagar and Evans.

#381 Making Contact

S: Isn't it scary how TV has become very much like the parodies of Future TV of the 80's and 90's (think RoboCop)? Was it Nature or Nurture? N: I'd buy that for a dollar!

What would you consider a sign that Earth just isn't quite ready yet

TV commercial quality issues, ... *not to mention the pop-up banner ads.* 8%

Senior Management of the planet needs refreshing, ... *I'm refreshing their heads!* 25%

Linux still not considered an Official Religion, ... *but I think it's the official OS of the Jedi though.* 7%

The Happy Mac's forced retirement, ... *he wasn't retired, he was abducted by aliens!* 15%

Wesley Crusher's scene being cut out of new Star Trek movie, ... *but I thought Star Trek X, Jaguar would have all the old features!* 14%

The Joy of Tech still not available in holo-book format, ... *that's just on Earth, due to those pesky Interplanetary JoT Regions.* 16%

What, you mean they didn't contact you yet? 13%

May not add up to exactly 100% due to rounding and JoyPoll Time Dilation.

#454 The Force Forecast

S: The cartoon form of George Lucas first made an appearance in AY2K, performing a puppet show version of Star Wars II. Because he is the Emperor of Marketing, our little in joke was to have him wearing Geek Culture t-shirts. I suppose we really should send him a Glow in the Dark Alien t-shirt sometime.

What's your Force Forecast?

A long period of good Force is about to come to an end, ... *hopefully along with those long scenes of Jedi romance.* 3%

Luminous weather have we, ... *are you sure it's not all that Dark Side lightning?* 11%

The Force is always brighter on the other side of the planet, ... *Q. Why did the Chewbacca cross the planet?* 8%

Don't forget to bring your lightsaber if you go out today, ... *is that your lightsaber, or are you just glad to see me?* 19%

The Dark Side clouds everything, ... *that's just an excuse those lazy Jedi use.* 20%

Weather is for Sithies. No mystical energy field controls my destiny, ... *it's not nice to ignore Emperor Nature!* 24%

I'm a storm trooper 12%

May not add up to exactly 100% due to rounding and I thought it smelled bad on the outside.

#290 First Contact

S: Nitrozac has always wanted to start her own Vulcan school, teaching logical thinking. N: Yes, it would be great fun to practice your poker face while pointing out how illogical everyone else is.

What event would cause the Vulcans to visit you?

Actually getting the pizza for free because it's late, ... *your odds of a free pizza will increase if you get a Klingon to answer the door.* 4%

Getting all my work done and on time, ... *now that's science fiction!* 16%

Making it through a whole day without crashing my computer, ... *maybe you need a visit from Tux, or the People from Planet X?* 4%

Cracking the RC5 code and winning that $1000.00 after I joined the GeekCulture Team, ... *half the fun is getting there, especially with all those other strange life forms on the team.;)* 4%

The event already happened and was so good, I didn't need those visiting Vulcans, ... *maybe they did arrive, but were too embarrassed when they got there.* 10%

It is illogical to think that Vulcans would ever visit me, ... *it is irrational for you to limit your imagination with such thinking.* 48%

I'm insisting the Vulcans visit first, then I'll vote. 11%

May not add up to exactly 100% due to rounding and I'm a cartoonist not a mathematician!

#208 Nomad water cooler

N: No, it doesn't mean sterilize the water, it means sterilize the human, as in kill him! Hmm, I'm suddenly thirsty. S: I wonder if he will eventually have to use Kirk's "sterilize your own imperfections" logic on the H2001.... "Telling me to get back to work prevents you from working." IF I'M NOT WORKING, I MUST BE DEFECTIVE... STERILIZE!

What would you program your H2001 to do?

Sterilize my cubicle, ... *perhaps start by emptying the garbage cans occasionally.* 3%

Swear, ... *an oath of allegiance I hope.* 10%

Spit, ... *it's something a squirt like you would do. ;)* 2%

Serve martinis, ... *sterilized, not stirred.* 39%

Serve Man, ... *goes down well with a glass of Earth water I hear.* 13%

Self-Destruct, ... *Code 000 Destruct 0.* 17%

I sterilized my vote. 13%

May not add up to exactly 100% due to rounding and the ultimate achievement in computer evolution.

AY2K #131, Alien Tricks

S: This was one of our favorite AY2Ks. I grew up reading my older brother's comic books, and always dreamed of getting some of those wacky items advertised in them. I eventually did get X-Ray Specs... and why yes, of course they worked!   N: mmm, soylent green gum.

What's the coolest thing about aliens?

Their hardware, ... *well of course, they've had a billion years lead development time!* 12%

Their soft, pliable, and hairless green skin, ... *just like Gumby's!* 5%

Their au natural fashion sense, ... *just like Pokey!* 14%

Despite their ability to go almost anywhere in the Universe, they've choosen to hang around me and my friends, ... *proof they are advanced life forms!* 32%

The fact that at least one of them is excited about going to Abacus World Expo, ... *and all advanced life forms love a good geek fest!!* 18%

I still yearn for one of those cardboard polaris nuclear submarines. 16%

May not add up to exactly 100% due to rounding and lost time while reading comic books.

#470 Event Horizon Café

S: Of course, to get this joke you need to know a bit about black holes, and how as an object gets closer to an event horizon, its time seems to slow down to an outside observer. Don't think about it too much though, or you'll soon realize that tidal forces would prevent you from ever sipping on an Event Horizon Café milkshake. N: What do you think they ordered... an Orange Crush and a Crunchy bar?

Besides taking forever to get an order, what else would you find annoying about the Event Horizon Cafe?

Once you go in, it seems you can never leave, ... *isn't that the Hotel California Effect?* 14%

It just doesn't have much of an atmosphere, ... *it's the kind of place that just sucks the energy right out of you.* 11%

I hate the singularity bar scene, ... *everyone's crushing together all the time.* 16%

I like my Space/Time shaken, not curved, ... *you might wanna try the drive-thru over at the Ejection Jet Burger Joint.* 24%

I hear someone found a wormhole in the Cosmic Soup, ... *they may have been tidally stretching the truth.* 7%

That darn accretion disk dirt gets everywhere, ... *are those messy particles a result of vacuum fluctuations?* 12%

I'm viewing the redshifted results. 13%

May not add up to exactly 100% due to rounding and that pesky Hawking radiation.

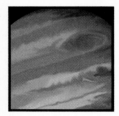

#170 The Nature of Jupiter

S: The geek man who asks annoying questions makes several appearances in JoT. Did you realize he has a son?... (as seen in JoT #119.) N: I wonder how he popped the question to his wife? "You wouldn't happen to be of breeding age and without a mate, would you?"

What do you think the lecture's title is?

A Weatherman's Guide to Jupiter, ... *his Weatherman's Guide to the Moon was really boring.* 5%

"Simply put," a guide to Simplifying Everything, ... *he's an advocate of the Simpleton Movement.* 20%

Gas Giants I know and love, ... *at least he's over his obsession with Uranus.* 17%

My Alien Abduction, and the photos they let me take, ... *the aliens finally had enough after he insisted they visit the tourist traps on Io.* 15%

2001, a Trailer Park Odyssey, ... *the part where the monkey tosses up a beer bottle is pretty cool.* 29%

I'm simply viewing the results. 11%

May not add up to exactly 100% due to rounding and getting lectured.

Favorite Destination

S: This is a comic we've been wanting to do for a long time now, but never seemed to find the time to finish. Hmmm, maybe our future selves finally got around to sending it to us! N: If I remember correctly, my past self worked pretty hard on it!
You can do the JoyPoll for this comic, ...exclusively for those who have this book! Find it online here...
http://www.joyoftech.com/joyoftech/thebestofjot/index.html

#306 Alien Roadshow

N: This comic was inspired by the Antique Roadshow television series... the British version's soundtrack has the strange effect of knocking Snaggy into unconsciousness. It would be neat if sometime in the future, this book appeared on an Antique Roadshow. S: And even cooler if it appeared on an Alien Roadshow!

How would you be categorized by an Alien race?

100 percent Grade "A" Geek, ... *does the A stand for Alpha or Asinine? ;)* 15%

Worthy of further observation, ... *have they checked out your webcam?* 15%

A fascinating little bug, ... *ironically, a geek becomes what he usually squashes.* 15%

An important part of this planet's ecology, ... bottom *feeders usually are. ;)* 4%

A worker drone, ... *as opposed to a slacker drone?* 10%

Pet food, ... *so you're kind of an ALPO geek?* 24%

I had a close encounter with the results. 13%

May not add up to exactly 100% due to rounding and 100% not equaling exactly 100% in other parts of the galaxy.

#267 Segway evolution

S: Sometimes it feels like the Macintosh made my legs obsolete. N: You're forgetting about our old sneakernet, where we had to share files via Zip disks. That kept you moving around a bit.   S: So, in actuality, it was the Ethernet network that made my legs obsolete!

How do you feel about the future depicted in this cartoon?

It represents a dangerous trend towards the loss of our physical selves, ... *it started in the year 404.* 25%

I can't wait! Please, cryogenic suspension now, ... *quit being such a cryonic baby about it.* 3%

I still want a Segway Human Transporter, despite the risks to humanity's future, ... *repeat after me... it's not a scooter, it's not a scooter.* 24%

My body is already pretty useless, so I'd really like one of those flying petri dishes, ... *were they invented by Rob Petri?* 31%

In the future, people will just view the results. 13%

May not add up to exactly 100% due to rounding and a billion tears.

Do you think I'm Xexy?

#431 Think Big

N: These would be great computers for Red Giants! S: Be careful when hanging around Red Giants... they can get pretty cranky after collapsing from burnout!

What would you do if you had a planet-sized laptop?

Drool an ocean, ... would you call it the Spit-cific Ocean? 2%

Call it MacWorld, ... *hopefully it's inhabited by Techno-Talking Babes.* 19%

Colonize, ... *be careful, those keyboard continents can get pretty inhospitable.* 15%

Put it in orbit and show DVDs to the entire world, ... *they call that a Super Drive-in!* 29%

Surf the whole World Wide Web on the weeelly weeelly wide scween, ... *hopefully, you'd share it wid the widdle wabbit too?* 8%

Take a few Charles Atlas courses so I could carry it around, ... *so instead of making a man out of Mac, the Mac made a man out of you?* 8%

I'd make it an reserve for Expo bears. 15%

May not add up to exactly 100% due to rounding and isostatic adjustment.

449 Klingon Mac Users

N: I think a combination MUG meeting and Star Trek convention would be really cool. I went to a ST con a few years ago. It was fun, but I was kinda creeped out by someone selling their sexual fantasy drawings of STTNG characters in porno positions. Snaggy sat beside a guy who inspired the animation in our Geek TV section of the website, called "Snot Trek". Ewwww!

Which Star Trek alien race do you think would most likely use Macs?

Klingons, ... to crash with honor is the hope of all great warriors. 2%

The Ferangi, ... how would the Ferangi feel about the free software movement? 4%

The Vulcans, ... is using Macs logical or illogical? 27%

The Borg, ... resistance is futile, prepare to use Jaguar. 5%

Those green skinned Orion Slave Girls, ... oh they use Mac alright, and Mac doesn't mind a bit. 7%

The Redmonds, ... aren't they just a result of a Borg/Ferangi crossbreeding experiment? Less than 1%

None of them, it's the future, ... hey, I thought the future was suppose to be optimistic. 12%

All of them, or at least those that are advanced life forms, ... I think different, therefore I am advanced? 24%

I'm too busy fighting a Gorn to vote 16%

May not add up to exactly 100% due to rounding and The Drake Equation.

#360 Speilberg's Pitch

N: I can just imagine a Speilberg-directed keynote, complete with eternally long close-ups of stunned faces as they try and take in the shocking reality of the new hardware. That would be –yawn– really exciting. S: And how would that be any different from a normal Expo?

What would be the best thing about a Spielberg MacWorld Expo keynote?

oooooo pretty lights, ... *those aren't special effects, it's a kernel panic!* 13%

The intense close-ups on faces with mouths agape, ... *what out for all that geeky drool!* 6%

The demo by Tom Cruise, ... *he's demoing his new SIM expansion pack "Doh! I got a Divorce".* 8%

The ET cameo, ... *darn it, those rumors sites said it would be Drew Barrymore!* 9%

His announcement of the "Jaws" docklett, ... *so realistic, you'll never feel safe in Aqua again!* 8%

George Lucas wouldn't be directing it, ... *awww, you mean Jar Jar won't be running the showdown?... Meesa CRASH!* 40%

I'm voting when it's on DVD. 13%

May not add up to exactly 100% due to rounding and Close Encounters of the Reality Distortion Kind.

#278 Michael Dell's Nightmare

S: Are Dell pillowcases a built-to-order option at Sears? N: Yes, but the cost really adds up if you order the satin edge trim and the 200 thread count!

What do you expect from MacWorld Expo?

A new iMac, that's about it, ... *you probably shouldn't have left the keynote early.* 6%

A new iMac and an iWalk PDA!, ... *did the iWalk rumor come from a Probably Distorted Advocate?* 8%

Something I really want but can't afford, ... *if you want it, it will come. It may just be last year's model by then.* 38%

I expect to be blown away, ... *just don't fall to pieces if it's another iLetdown.* 13%

I expect to be devastated, ... *I'm devastated that I'm not expected!* 3%

I'm still holding out for Abacus World Expo, ... *Abacus, not Abs World Expo!* 9%

I'm expecting another amazing poll question. 20%

May not add up to exactly 100% due to rounding and iHype distortion fields.

#341 Mac Cruise

S: This comic was suggested by David Pogue in an email sent from the Mac Cruise ship. We knew we had captured the essence of the cruise when, after seeing the finished comic, he emailed back..."*LOL!! ABSOLUTELY FREAKIN' PERFECT!!! Oh my god!... and it's so true!...Now I'm laughing more, going crazy.. HOW DID YOU KNOW ABOUT THE DOLPHIN SCULPTURE IN THE POOL!?!? ... David*" Heh, ... if we told you, we'd have to delete you.   N: I'm waiting for the HaX0r Cruise to watch the antics ensue as they hack everything from slot machines to ship navigation. Hee hee. S: They could advertise it as the Un-crackable Titanic. I hope you're planning to watch from a lifeboat! Hmmm, thanks to this comic, if I ever go on a cruise and they don't have a David Pogue and the Poguettes Broadway Review, I'll be pretty disappointed.

How many different "things to do" does the comic portray?

Billions and Billions, ... *does Mac Mania offer Butt-head Astronomer lessons?* 5%

3.14159265..., ... *is it true that the Babble-ons first started the pi craze?* 6%

It depends how friendly the pool babes are, ... *that depends on how broken your Base Station is.* 43%

One. Everyone knows David Pogue and the Poguettes is the only show in town, ... *Pogue's Reviews are legendary!* 5%

None. The AirPort Base Station is broken, ... *oh man, is that All your Base Station?* 11%

Where'd Woz go?, ... *you need a Wheels of Zeus device to keep track of him nowadays.* 14%

I'm at the buffet eating Pi. 12%

May not add up to exactly 100% due to rounding and the Poguettes's precision synchronization.

#283 David Pogue's Nightmare

N: Hopefully for David's sake, those lost manuals will never be found. I bet they're hiding out in Atlantis. S: Don't you find it a really strange coincidence that shortly after those original manuals went missing, David came out with his own series of books... hmmmm...

What would be your worst nightmare?

Having to read manuals, ... *you mean you don't curl up in bed with them?* 11%

Having to write manuals, ... *so you don't like doing manual labor?* 26%

Having to write the Missing Manual on Nightmares, ... *just wait until you meet your editor!* 7%

Being stranded on a desert island, without any David Pogue reading material, ... *so you'd be missing the Missing Manual?* 7%

A missing teddy bear, ... *he's not missing, he probably just went to Vegas.* 15%

Not having OS X, since I can't see those David Pogue icons in their full glorious size, ... *size doesn't usually matter, except in this case.* 17%

What would be your worst nightmare? (*continued*)

Having to choose just one of the above was my nightmare. 14%

May not add up to exactly 100% due to rounding and not having a poll manual.

BEZOS, CALM DOWN! I'M SURE DAVID HAS A GOOD EXPLANATION FOR THIS... HOLD ON A SEC...

DAMN IT POGUE, *WAKE UP* AND ANSWER YOUR PHONE!

#389 Happy Mac Karoke

N: I had some pretty big issues with the removal of the Happy Mac. It was awful! I miss that little happy face like you wouldn't believe. S: What? You mean a white corporate logo staring at you during boot-up isn't giving you the warm and fuzzies?   yeah, I miss it too, I really do think it was responsible for Mac users seeing their machines as companions.

What do you passionately whine about?

Happy Mac getting sacked, ... *oh the inhumanity!* 4%

dotMac, therefore iWhine, ... *they think different, therefore they pay.* 10%

The whining of my coworkers, ... *so that's what that whining noise is!* 6%

Not having a significant other, ... *lesson #1, whining is NOT an aphrodisiac.* 18%

It has to do with Windows, ... *have you tried Wine?* 24%

I'm a whine-free zone, ... *believe me, everyone is whining about your whine-free zone!* 21%

Awwww, all the good stuff to whine about is already taken! 12%

May not add up to exactly 100% due to rounding and incessancy.

#363 Think Wild!

S: This comic features Nitro's magnificent drawing of Edith Prickly, Andrea Martin's character on the legendary SCTV television program. N: Did you notice when Apple brought out the Jaguar theme, that suddenly everything in stores was covered in jaguar patterns? It also happened with the colorful iMacs. I think you could furnish your entire house with a bondi blue iMac theme.

What's your favorite animal print object?

Edith Prickley, station manager for SCTV, ... her station programming plan was "boobs, bums, good-looking hunky guys, and no more sports"... *hey, wasn't that our schedule for AY2K? ;)* 5%

My car seat covers, ... *can you tell a lemon by its spots?* 1%

A certain bikini, ... *sounds like you're the animal!* 39%

My fine-grained multithreading, UNIX-based operating system, ... *but I thought cats didn't like Aqua!* 21%

Without a doubt, it's my "Think Wild" poster/t-shirt/etc. I'm buying today, ... *it works out to less than a cent for every time you'll laugh your apples off looking at it.* 1%

I'm more of a plant print person, ... *you've been wearing hemp lately, haven't you?* 14%

My fave is "Fluffy," and I'm not going to tell you what "Fluffy" is. 15%

May not add up to exactly 100% due to rounding and faux math.

#281 The new iMac

N: You know, when you see it in person, that round base is huge, ...it's an igloo! A basket of kittens could live in there! S: Um, do baskets of kittens normally live in igloos?

What would you call the new iMac?

An abomination, ... *since it's white, would that make it an abominable abomination?* 14%

The Sorcerer's Appendage, ... *that sounds like a really bad porn movie.* 25%

The Pleasure Dome, ... *you can burn your own movies with it.* 15%

Friend, colleague, lover, ... *you really do have sex in "The City" on your mind lately, don't you!* 14%

The new San Francisco Treat, ... *alright all Roni, I get your drift!* 10%

Lust-o-Lamp, ... *is that like the Geek Culture Eroto-Cam?* 30%

The Power P C-Cup, ... *bet you can't wait to get your hands on one.* 28%

I don't call the new iMac, it calls me. 33%

May not add up to exactly 100% due to rounding, and being able to move it with one finger.

406 Jobbie Jaguar's Mac O's

S: A fan, Glen Warner, suggested the Mac O's idea to us, and we thought it was pretty funny. Picking up on the cereal box theme, we developed the Jobbie Jaguar character. N: Then I became obsessed with vintage cereal box design, and collecting box tops for the Lone Ranger fan club buttons! S: Hi Ho Jobbie, away!

What's your favorite Hi Tech Cereal?

Jobby the Jaguar's insanely great Mac O's, ... *Got Aqua?* 32%

Redmond Bran, ... *helps regulate those other Microsoft products.* 1%

Linus the Lionhearted's Crispy Kernels, ... *fyi, a real cereal... do you think Linus was named after it?* 12%

I have sweet spot for Cap'n Crunch, ... *just don't blow the whistle on him!* 15%

FrankenBallmer's Flailing Flakes, ... *good for developing, developing, developing minds!* 3%

Snap! Crackle! and Static, ... *free wrist strap in every box!* 6%

I can't get enough of those Silicon Chips, ... *sorry Granny, I just can't resist those big puffs of wheat tumbled through hot sugar and honey.* 13%

I'm just counting my Lucky Charms. 15%

May not add up to exactly 100% due to rounding and the Cupertino Raisins.

#445 Reefer Madness

N: Seconds after the news broke that the Dell Dude was arrested for possession of marijuana, millions of Mac fans cheered at the thought they might never again have to hear him say the dreaded... "Doooood, you're getting a Dell." S: Jessycat knew the girlfriend of Benjamin Curtis, (the actor who portrays the Dell Dude), and had the pleasure of meeting him one night. She admitted to being a little starstruck. Luckily his Dell Distortion Field wasn't too strong... she bought a PowerBook a few months later.

What is your new favorite Dudeism?

Dude, you're getting a cell, ... *he may have lost a few brain cells in the process though.* 31%

Dude, pass the bong, ... *that's not a bong, it's a 40 gig Windows iPod!* 10%

Officer, you're getting a Dude, ... *but Officer, you can't arrest me, I'm a Joy of Tech celebrity!* 11%

Yes your honor, thank you your honor, ... *you're looking lovely today Mrs. Cleaver.* 9%

Dude, any publicity is good publicity, ... *especially if it gets you into a comic!* 3%

Dude, never wear a kilt if there's a chance you might spend the night in jail, ... *Dude, you shoulda asked the Kilt Genius.* 18%

I'm just viewing the results... *bummer.* 14%

May not add up to exactly 100% due to rounding and a round up.

#370 Mona Switcher

S: Ellen Feiss was one of Apple's Switchers, and her "stone-faced" performance in her commercial won her instant Internet celebrity. Nitrozac had a theory that the real reason Ellen's eyes were bloodshot was due to a long photo shoot under bright studio lights.... Um, sure Nitro... that and all the smoke in the room!

What would be your favorite painting from Nitrozac's Tech series?

Mona Switcher (Ellen Feiss), ... *dudette, you're switching from DELL.* 14%

The Birth of Apple, ... *is that Woz rising out of the clamshell?* 5%

The Last Pizza Slice, ... *is that a religious piece, or a battlefield painting?* 3%

The TTB Nymphs, ... *art is a great excuse to look at naked babes!* 38%

Blue Boy Vs Kasparov, ... *now there's a Deep Thought.* 2%

Tux crossing into Richmond, ... *painted about the same time as "Bill Gates' Scream."* 7%

Return of the Prodigal Steve Jobs, ... *forms a nice diptic with "Amelio's Last Stand."* 10%

I'm more into Nitrozac's movie posters. 18%

May not add up to exactly 100% due to rounding and mathematics thinner.

#313 X-Birthday

N: Hopefully this won't turn out to be the kind of holiday that makes everyone depressed.   S: Shortly after this comic was uploaded, Forum member crazyarlo sent us this email... "Just saw your newest cartoon, and had to let you know....I did this at work!!! My wife thought I was nuts, but hey, it's the FIRST BIRTHDAY OF OSX, DAMMIT!! I got lots of chances to talk to my PC using friends, explain what OSX is, etc. Mostly they came for the cake."

What tech anniversary would you like to celebrate?

My first boot-up, ... *I didn't know you liked skiing so much!* 10%

Jobs' return to Apple, ... *an insanely great ascension?* 23%

The release of Windows 95, ... *where do you want to celebrate today?* 2%

The birth of Linux, ... *what about Tux's birthday?* 16%

The birth of the Apple I, ... *you gotta love that Homebrew!* 10%

That whole day I didn't crash, ... *something tells me you aren't celebrating the birth of Linux or OS X enough.* 22%

I'm celebrating the results. 15%

May not add up to exactly 100% due to rounding and the noise from the people next door celebrating DOS Day.

#465 A Panther Cam-pain

N: Remember that keynote where Steve Jobs got mad at the digital camera and just tossed it like an empty pop can? Ouch. That musta hurt.
S: A fan, Brian, wrote us after seeing this one..."I just had to write in and say THANK YOU for the PINK DIFFERENT cartoon! It made me laugh so hard at my desk that I started to cry!!!!! HELP ME!!!! Thanks for the GREAT JOB!!!" Thank *you* Brian!

What's your favorite feature of OS X Pink Panther?

The pink fur desktop theme, ... *but not a real pink fur desktop, that's cruel.* 4%

Sherlock replaced by Inspector Clouseau, ... *so finding stuff is now officially A Shot in the Dark?* 32%

Default Speech Voice now "Peter Sellers," ... *how can you have millions of default voices?* 9%

Start-up chime replaced by Henry Mancini's "Da doot da doo, da doot....," ... *da doot da doot da doo da doot, da doooooo ....* 18%

The free upgrade, ... *heh, now there's a shot in the dark!* 17%

I just hope it's not a bumbling OS, ... *Does yer OS crash? / No. / Nice OS... *crash!!* ... I thought you said yer OS did not crash! / Zat iz not my OS!* 5%

I'm waiting for Mac OS X Columbo. 12%

May not add up to exactly 100% due to rounding and the ant and the aardvark.

#482 Teach the world to sing.

S: Sometimes we'll get an email that will really make our day or week.   This is a snippet of one of those, written shortly after we posted this comic...
"this is the best one ever!! I sang it out loud, - did you know you can sing and smile at the same time! -halting momentarily along the way as my voice cracked as the laughter came through! Absolutely delightful. The pictures are wonderful and the words so clever. Genius. Genius. Thank you Thank you Thank you. (It's been a rough couple of months in my life and yesterday felt especially hard; the delightful cleverness of your creation has me smiling still. You made my day way better.) - Jill

I'd like to teach the world to...?

Sing, ... *as long as you don't sing, sing it loud, sing it strong, your whole life long.* 1%

Smile, ... *at least smiles don't cost 99 cents.* 4%

Suffer, ... *you mean, you're going to sing to us? ;)* 7%

Think, ... *the world thinks, just not the way you'd like it to.* 28%

Think Different, ... *don't you think it's time for a different slogan?* 30%

Those who can, do. Those who can't, teach, ... *if only that rule applied to some singers. ;)* 17%

You can learn a lot by observing the results. 9%

May not add up to exactly 100% due to rounding and imperfect harmony.

#459 What if Jobs was one of us?

S: To be sung to the tune of (What if God was) One of Us" made popular by Joan Osborne, written by Eric Bazilian. We had a great response to this comic, and several people continued the rhyming in the Forums. Superflippy added "Yeah, yeah, Jobs is great. Yeah, yeah, Aqua's good." perfectstormy added "Nobody calls him on the phone...'cept for The Woz from his new home." The Joypoll features variations of many of our Forum members nicks...

If Jobs had a nick, what would it be?

Snup Jobbie Job, ... or perhaps Skyjobs, or Steve-ungo? 7%

Twinkle Jobs, ... or JobbieGoddess, or RDFJOBS, PB? 2%

Jobbiecat, ... or perhaps Jobcat, or Evil Jobbie? 7%

LostInCupertino, ... or Swiss MacMercenary, or SteenJobs, or ZwilSteve_nik? 11%

Jobnevik, ... or SteveSpielgel, or ilovemyRealityDistortionField? 2%

Jobsman97, ... or maybe SteveMx, or iSteveJobsdesign? 3%

Cap'n Macintosh, ... or supaJobs, or Alien Jobvestor? 20%

DigitalJobs, ... or JobsMaster, or neotatsteve? 3%

Jobs, the Wizard of, ... not to be confused with the Wizard of Woz. 13%

ZorroTheJobs, ... or jobmatic, or maybe cheezie jobs? 2%

A variation of MY nick, ... so many nicks, so little JoyPoll options! 6%

I'm going to go register for the Forums 17%

May not add up to exactly 100% due to rounding and twinkle twinkle little Jobs, how I wonder what you're working on.

Geek Culture

#367 Keyboard Bitching Session

N: Be nice to your keyboard, I treat mine to a rubdown of isopropyl alcohol every once in a while. Snaggy's keyboard—that's another story! S: I am guided by the Prime Directive... I have pledged not to disturb the lifeforms that live on my keyboard until they discover warp drive.

What's your favorite keyboard party hourderve?

Keys and crackers, ... serve them and your guests will be phreaking out! 5%

Chips, of course, ... no thanks, I have to cut down on my silicon. 16%

Breadboard, ... socket to me! 8%

Qwerty little bits and bytes, ... do they go snap, crackle and click-a-dee click? 13%

What's your favorite keyboard party hourderve? (*continued*)

Keyboard party! Nope, I ain't the type, ... you always were a killjoy stick. 21%

This comic is offensive to Wacom, ... perhaps, but what a font-astic poll! 18%

I'm trackballing the results. 15%

May not add up to exactly 100% due to rounding and the ALT vs Command Feud.

486 The Nerd Club

S: On our Forums, Tech Angel wondered – "What kind of dictionary has the "b" words in the middle? Hmm-m...perhaps it's an English/Spanish (or whatever) dictionary and he's translating on the fly. Or maybe it's not a dictionary at all, but a ??? The mind reels..... BTW, I love his socks."

What would be your favorite thing at The Nerd Club?

The dictionary readings, ... I love rhyming dictionary karaoke night! 3%

The bar made out of old slide rules, ... yes, of course they made it so you could still use them! 14%

The emergency eyeglass repair kit, ... with three kinds of tape! 5%

Watching the spelling bee competitions on the big screen TV, ... it's the sound system that is truly a-w-e-s-o-m-e. 6%

When the rival debating clubs come in and trade objections, ... watch out, if things get any more heated, they're gonna need that eyeglass repair kit! 8%

Duh...the waitresses, ... I thought it was just geeks who fell in love with servers! 52%

Protest vote over depiction of socializing nerds. 9%

May not add up to exactly 100% due to rounding and exhaustive definitions.

#323 Blog Poll

N: The web poll is the perfect choice for those who can't make a decision on their own. Hmmm, now, what should I have for lunch? a) soup b) sandwich c) soup and sandwich d) microwave meal. Hurry! I'm getting hungry! S: Heh... May not add up to rounding and a Snaggy in the kitchen.

So what do you think, should she stay with him or dump him?

Stay with him, ... after all, that predating agreement seemed fair. 9%

Dump him, ... I wouldn't blame her, after that Christmas present fiasco. 3%

She should stay with him until the bill is paid, then dump him, ... he should have negotiated an extended warranty. 12%

This is something between her and him, I don't want to be involved, ... if you didn't want to be involved, you shouldn't have been listening in on their conversation. ;) 28%

So what do you think, should she stay with him or dump him? (*continued*)

She should wait for the final results of this poll, ... *she'd better watch out, he's a geek. He might have a script running.* 30%

I'm checking out his blog for the dirt on her! 14%

May not add up to exactly 100% due to rounding and breaking up in a public place.

#353 Blogging Someone

N: And soon he will be blogging about her blogging someone else. S: His hits are going to go way down!

How do you describe the way you communicate with your Significant Other?

Dial up, ... *hopefully you're not getting those busy signals.* 2%

We have a Peer to Peer relationship, ... *hopefully you're sharing more than files.* 16%

We SMTP use email, ... *let's hope you don't have to MIME often.* 1%

Point to Point Protocol, ... *hopefully not Point VS Point.* 6%

A T1 line connects our souls, ... *a T3 to your TTB?* 12%

Lately we've had our firewalls up, ... *maybe you should deliver a packet or two?* 6%

I'm attempting to establish a connection, ... *keep on ping'in, try not to timeout.* 38%

I'm using a sniffer. 15%

May not add up to exactly 100% due to rounding and not giving a fraggle.

#365 Wil Wheaton's Run

N: Wil Wheaton is a really sensitive guy and isn't ashamed to cry and blog about being sensitive and crying while blogging. Awwww. S: Hey, I cried during that Star Trek "Wesley is a Traveller" episode!

What's your favorite part of Wil Wheaton's Run, the movie?

The computer-breeded humans who live only for the pleasure of blogging, ... *that part was way too real for comfort.* 2%

The deadly ritual of Carrousel, where bloggers are reborn to blog out another fun and pleasure-filled 30 years of inputting text, ... *at least it's better than having to read them for the next 30 years.* 2%

Sanctuary, the Land of Unlimited Free Bandwidth, ... *enjoy it while it lasts, it's going to cost 99 bucks soon.* 20%

What's your favorite part of Wil Wheaton's Run, the movie? (*continued*)

The dream sequence where Wesley Crusher is executed to make way for the next generation, ... *I knew that was a dream, especially since Wil was playing the executioner.* 15%

The dream sequence where I'm making out with Farrah Fawcett, ... *you'd have a better chance of outrunning a Sandman.* 24%

That cool blinking crystal in my left hand, ... *on your mark, get set, ... RUN!!!!!* 17%

I'm seeking Sanctuary. 16%

May not add up to exactly 100% due to rounding and where there's a Wil, there's a way.

#387 Ornery Geeks

N: Oh how I envy you Young Ornery Geek! You have your whole life to come back with witty quips that fly over the heads of the dull and ignorant. Ah, to be young again! S: He also has his whole life to be made fun at and teased by jocks.

What happened next?

A fist travelling at high velocity collided with an ornery geeklette cheek, ... *no, not his bum cheek... jeese!* 11%

The geeklette, continuing to drone on and on, rendered the other kid unconscious, ... *it's his super power.* 8%

The other kid's parents arrived, and marveled how their kid was becoming a bully, just like them, ... *then proceeded to pick on the ornery Geeks.* 16%

The family gave each other a group hug and proceeded to lineup for Star Wars Episode III, ... *then they pretended to light-sabre fight, each perfecting their own personal light-sabre sound.* 3%

The geeklette's father turned to the mother and said, "Well, you know dear, I'm not surprised in the least that you'd say that, ... but you have to admit, Anakin is lame.", ... *then she said, "don't get me started about that Amidala bitch!"* 22%

The mother and father smiled at the young man, then transformed into balls of light energy and said in a booming voice..."Captain Kirk, perhaps there is hope for your race, we will spare your planet from destruction.", ... *as geeks, I needn't remind you that the preceding scene would be highly unlikely in a comic based on the characters and events of Star Wars, however not outside the realm of science fiction.* 23%

I'm not surprised in the least that you viewed the results. 13%

May not add up to exactly 100% due to rounding and lame mathematics.

#021 Support group for ISP Abuse

N: Boy, can we relate to this one! A couple of times our web host in Atlanta lost our server... yep, they could not physically locate our server! We were on the verge of booking flights to Atlanta to help with the search-and-rescue. /me crosses fingers. /me knocks on wood.

You can do the JoyPoll for this comic, ...exclusively for those who have this book! Find it online here...
http://www.joyoftech.com/joyoftech/thebestofjot/index.html

#437 Extremely Easy Rider

N: The biggest thrill of my humble career as a techie cartoonist was meeting Woz, the legend of Silicon Valley, and finding a brilliant, warm, kind, and funny human being. And being able to give just a little something back, to teach his students a bit about cartooning... that was just awesome!

Recently, Woz sent some movies of him and his friends joyriding on Segways. They were having a blast, chasing, racing, adjusting the handlebars for knee riding, and always, always laughing. They were having fun, they were in geek glee, they were unbridled joy as they were playing with Segways. That's when it hit me, that Woz IS the joy of tech.

Sometimes we get so stressed out by technology, and the best medicine for this is laughter.

What would be your favorite scene in Extremely Easy Rider?

Those amazing riding down the wide-open sidewalk scenes, ... *cross-country at 12 mph, soft breeze in your hair!* 4%

The Steppenwolf songs, ... *my faves, "Born to be Kinda Wild", and "God Damn Jeff Bezos".* 11%

The smashup derby between the Hummer and Segway, ... *it was almost as short a scene as Bambi VS Godzilla.* 12%

The love scene between Dean and Ginger, ... *um, was LSD involved?* 2%

The part where the redneck villagers club Jeff Bezos to death like a baby seal, ... *don't get too excited, it's only a movie!* 23%

All those hot Segway biker chicks, ... *those aren't biker chicks, those are Segway grannies!* 35%

If this Segway's a' rocking, I'm not a' walking. 11%

May not add up to exactly 100% due to rounding and two wheels are better than one.

#385 Dell Rumors

S: Have you ever had one of those brilliant ideas that is going to change the world and make you rich, and then it dawns on you that it just could be the Stupidest Idea Ever™? N: You really should patent that!

What would be your favorite part of the Dell Rumors website?

The chance that His Dell-ness might actually be reading it, ... *did you say his Dull-ness?* 1%

DELL's Legal team sending in rumor suggestions, ... *they are very innovative in that way.* 18%

The "Switchers are Traitors!" editorial, ... *the Ellen Feise dartboard graphic went a little too far though.* 9%

The "Floppy Forever" items in the webstore, ... *I especially like the Floppy Forever! floppy labels for your floppies.* 11%

What would be your favorite part of the Dell Rumors website? (continued)

The exclusive, in-depth interview with the Dell Dude, ... *in-depth interview with the Dell Dude?... that's gotta be an oxymoron.* 13%

It's only a comic, it's only a comic, it's only a comic, ... *make sure you're clicking your boot disks together.* 31%

I much prefer HP Rumors! 14%

May not add up to exactly 100% due to rounding and things being easy as Dell.

#401 Pop-up Warrior

S: Pop-up ads suck, but when you are the owner of a website trying to survive financially, they sometimes become a necessary evil. Luckily they are really easy to turn off now in most browsers. N: But then you'll miss all those great opportunities to play Pop-up Warrior!

On the bright side, what's the best thing about pop-up ads?

They help improve my hand/eye co-ordination, ... *I thought that's what porn was for... ;)* 8%

They help me practice Tourette syndrome, ... *hopefully you don't have speech recognition software on.* 12%

They make me look like I'm multitasking, ... *hook up another mouse and go at it with both barrels.* 9%

In the right browser, they are relatively easy to turn off, ... *yes, but you'll never know what you're missing!* 38%

They introduce me to things I would never ever think of buying, ... *so in a way, they're very educational?* 6%

They provide essential revenue to the likes of Nitrozac and Snaggy, ... *essential revenue = NitroKitty's dinner.* 13%

I was aiming for a pop-up, but hit View the Results by mistake. 11%

May not add up to exactly 100% due to rounding and things popping up every now and then.

#197 Dates with Girls

N: Would you agree that Men are from Redmond and Women are from Cupertino? S: LOL.... Of course not!... < Warning. Fatal exception has occurred in module snaggy.dll>

What is your foolproof chick-attracting OS?

Unix, ... *ummm, you didn't say eunuchs did you?* 7%

OS X, ... *too bad it's pronounced "10", which is considerably less sexy than "X".* 17%

Windows, ... *the poll said foolproof chick attracting, not chickproof fool attracting!* 5%

Classic Mac OS, ... *is there not something sexy about unprotected memory?* 10%

What is your foolproof chick-attracting OS? (*continued*)

Linux, ... *a Tux doll has warmed many an open source babe's heart.* 23%

Some other semiobscure OS, ... *hey, a little mystery can be pretty hot.* 13%

I use my OS to attract hunks, ... *like they say, honey attracts more flies.* 6%

I have a hang up about OSs being sexy. 15%

May not add up to exactly 100% due to rounding and sensual mathematics.

#262 Beer User Group

N: BUG rivalry could be disasterous! There might be clashes between European BUGs and North American BUGs over whether beer should be served warm or cold, using up those valuable brain cells that should, by all rights, be sacrificed directly to beer. S: Everyone knows Canadian BUGs would be the world's best!   Actually, after the comic ran, I did get an email from a real BUG in Europe. Mmmmmm BUGs!

What would be the best thing about joining a beer user group?

The free-as-in-beer samples, ... *well, I'll have one for the principle of it.* 22%

The fascinating facts about beer one could learn while attending meetings, ... *almost as fun as reading the labels!* 4%

The door prizes, ... *just don't walk into the door on the way out.* 5%

Welcoming new members, ... *it's traditional for new members to get a round of advice.* 4%

Member discounts from local breweries, ... *but in European breweries, you still have to pay the VAT tax.* 19%

Being able to flash my Beer User Group membership card, ... *the police who stopped you would probably rather see your license.* 27%

My user group is already all about the beer. 15%

May not add up to exactly 100% due to rounding and I am Canadian.

AY2K #137   Geek Constellations

S: Creating the comic AY2K day after day, 7 days a week, really honed our skills. I like to call that stretch of time our "Hamburg Period"... exhausting, but exhilarating in many ways. N: AY2K fans were devoted beyond our expectations and they hold a special place in our hearts of gratitude. (The TTBs send their love.)

That's Fawn with the Geek! Where's Dawn?

She's all hopped up on Hawaiian with Dude, ... *oh oh, now they're breaking into his chocolate-covered Macadamia nuts!* 8%

She's hunting Internet Monkeys with Relic, ... *you see, the best time to hunt them is at night, when they are asleep in the money trees. That way they are very easy to net!* 9%

She's in bed with the other TTB's, ... *they're all asleep in their tent. Fawn's a real night owl!* 31%

She downed a few too many Slashdot cupcakes, ... *betcha can't eat just one!* 16%

She's working late at her portable Laboratory again, ... *she calls it her Porta-Labbie!* 34%

May not add up to exactly 100% due to rounding and astronomical calculations.

#419 Lord of the Root

N: The fine looking geek in this comic is maswan, longtime fan, and SuperFan. He's also a super fan of the Lord of the Rings. Maswan shared with us, on chat and the forums, his experiences and photos of camping out in front of the theater for the opening of LOTRs 2 in Sweden. Cool! S: Did you know that maswan is also the Official Geek Culture Baker? His cakes are the stuff of legend!

Which land are you the Lord of?

I'm the Wizard of Windowswaith, ... *with your faithful sidekick Clippy?* 4%

I am the Master of Mount Mac, ... *show me on a map... does X mark the spot?* 28%

Tuxador is my chosen land, ... *where the rivers are open source, and run like free beer?* 6%

Slacker-shire is where I rule, ... *do you rule with a slack fist?* 11%

I am Lord of the Root! One geek rules them all, ... *well, I did hear they were going to inherit the earth.* 16%

I'm pretty sure I live in the Land of Moron-dor, ... *hey, it wasn't me that called him a moron!* 19%

I'm Lording over my Land O'Lakes. 11%

May not add up to exactly 100% due to rounding and the Lord of the Rootabaga.

479 Girls Hate Math?

N: I could never understand why some people think that girls don't like math. You have to be a mathematician to figure out things like Body Mass Indexes, Optimal Heart Rates, and calorie contents of foods in order to be dieting like any normal weight-obsessed teen! S: Math skills are also very important for guys... especially when it comes to figuring out how much beer is necessary to achieve a desired blood alcohol level.

How are your math skills?

Infinitely good, ... *if good = infinite, is great = (infinity + 1)?* 16%

They were good, but recently have been subtracting, ... *so I guess you're thinking "what's the difference."* 17%

They are a fraction of what they used to be, ... *sounds like your denominator is dominating your numerator.* 24%

They've been multiplying, ... *that's exponentially cool.* 4%

poor < my math skills > great, ... *remember the alligator (or Pac-Man) always wants to eat the larger number.* 16%

They add up to... um, ... zero, ... *sounds like something isn't adding up!* 8%

Math girls are easy. 13%

May not add up to exactly 100% due to rounding and the sum being greater than the parts.

#092 Barbie's DotCom rescue

S: I have never seen anyone get so excited over software as the time when Nitrozac ran the Basket of Puppies simulation.   N: Actually, I think you were more excited over Barbie's Barely Legal Cousin.

What's your favorite part of Barbie, Dotcom Rescue?

The game where you work your employees to death, ... *warning, some scenes may be too familiar.* 6%

The part where you make the CEO explain the losses to the shareholders, ... *huh? You mean we're supposed to make a profit?* 28%

The part where Jeff Bezos gives me a medal, ... *it was almost as good as the Slashdotting Ceremony!* 4%

The part where the Media turns a boom into a bust, ... *they love those riches-to-rags stories.* 9%

Watching Barbie give her little pep talks, ... *is that why you're suddenly super turned on?* 25%

My cameo. I play myself, ... *was that you? I was sure it was William Shatner!* 15%

I viewed the results... *no one can look away from a crash.* 11%

May not add up to exactly 100% due to rounding and naming your own price.

#494 iChat /iSound

N: Think of online flatulence as an opportunity for couple bonding. Well, at least you can't smell it! S: You can if you're iChatting to each other in the same room, like true geeks will.

What do you blame your flatulence on?

My pet, ... *um, but I thought you had a pet rock?* 6%

I just sat on a whoopee cushion, ... *was it good for it too?* Less then 1%

It must be a bug in iChatAV, ... *would that be a stinkbug?* 17%

I'm a girl. We all know girls don't fart, ... *of course not, although I believe there are rumors of derrière exhalation.* 8%

Mine are so bad, New Zealand is going to tax me, ... *oh don't have a cow on me!* 14%

No excuses necessary... I'm silent and deadly, ... *if only that kind of ripping was illegal.* 36%

This poll stinks! 14%

May not add up to exactly 100% due to rounding and the bean counters eating their work.

#321 Adjustable Geek

N: I think this is a case of when someone starts to look like their pet. This guy just started to look like his beloved computer, he was spending so much time with it! S: Hmmm, so what then is the wife spending so much time with?

How's your posture today?

I'm sitting pretty, ... *is that your final position on this issue?* 18%

It'll get me over the hump, ... *by Wednesday, that hump is even bigger.* 5%

I've got a hunch it's not that great, ... *ok, but don't stick your neck out on my account.* 14%

I am a geek, posture is irrelevant, ... *sounds like you need some resistance training.* 36%

I have about as much posture as a potato, ... *baked, mashed, fried, or Tater Tot?* 11%

I'm too spineless to vote. 12%

May not add up to exactly 100% due to rounding and neck-and-neck results.

#457 Pop-Up Annoying Book Store Clerk

N: I must confess I sometimes go to Amazon and read the "Look inside" sections without any intention of buying anything, just like when I'm browsing in the book store in real life. It's fun! S: Note to person reading this right now in a bookstore.... Buy this book or we'll delete the geeks!

What would you find the most annoying?

Pop-up Annoying Book Store Clerk, ... *maybe someone could stop him with a bookworm.* 2%

Pop-up Overbearing Used Car Salesman, ... *how can I get you, in that car today?!* 9%

The completely ignore you when you need some Help Menu, ... *just keep clicking next.* 15%

Pop-over and cover-up Morality Inspector, ... *aka, your spying spouse.* 15%

The strip-search your hard drive Software Security Guard, ... *you won't mind, you've got nothing to hide, right?* 25%

The I'm talking on the phone you are invisible to me Tech Support Person, ... *well, work is the perfect time to plan your social life!* 16%

Can I help you find another poll option? 14%

May not add up to exactly 100% due to rounding and annoying percentages.

#441 Our Dreams Continue

N: This is our tribute to the astronauts who perished in the Columbia space shuttle tragedy. NASA geeks, their spirit and intellect, inspired me to create Geek Culture, way back when it was planned to be a CD-ROM, even before we started the website. It's amazing to learn about the extraordinary lives these astronauts and the control room geeks lead.
S: It's a difficult thing to do in many ways, expressing our feelings of such a tragedy into a Joy of Tech comic, but for us, it was too important an event (on many levels) to not do something, and creating such a work is a part of how we deal with our own feelings of heartbreak. Here are a couple of Forum posts that I though were appropriate...
Tech Angel posted: "Thank you, Nitrozac and Snaggy, for today's JoT. I was waiting to see your "take" on the Columbia disaster, expecting from past such tributes that you would provide us with a poignant message. You did not disappoint. I've heard the cartoon's sentiment echoed from several quarters in the past day-and-a-half, but not nearly as elegantly as you have here.
"A ship in the harbor is safe -- but that is not what ships are for." (John Shedd)
And so it is with humankind... Thanks again for the reminder."
skylar added: "...this JoT made me feel better by reminding me that the most fitting tribute to those that died would be to continue striving for the goal that was theirs."

What inspires you most to boldly go?

Science fiction, ... *those skimpy spacegirl outfits help too.* 14%

Science fact, ... *it's good to know you know you still don't know it all.* 12%

Life's Big Mysteries, ... *sometimes Life's Little Answers aren't the ones you were hoping to find.* 16%

The view from the shoulders of the giants we stand on, ... *at NASA, those giants are also pretty geeky.* 26%

The desire to boldly get, ... *just remember, a bird in your hand is sometimes not worth two you're still looking for.* 8%

I'm a boldly follower, ... *but as followers go, I'm sure you lead the pack.* 5%

I'm still looking for inspiration. 16%

May not add up to exactly 100% due to rounding and Math's sense of humor.

#418 Computer Geek, This was your Life

S: This is, of course, a tribute to the Jack Chick comics that terrorized me as a kid, and entertain me so much now a days. Is it just me or does anyone else think Jack gets his kicks living life vicariously through his comic characters? N: Kinda like us?

What will be the reaction to the movie of your life?

A hushed crowd, ... *are they hushed in awe or just asleep?* 3%

Polite clapping, ... *are you sure that's not wings flapping?* 9%

A cheering crowd, a standing ovation, ... *any chance for a sequel?* 5%

Angels will stumble out of the theatre saying "Huh? Did you get that?", ... *I guess you had to have read the book.* 42%

Do they throw tomatoes in Heaven, ... *all good tomatoes got to heaven, the rotten ones end up in the chilli pot of fire.* 12%

I'll be on hand to receive Hell's equivalent of an Academy Award, ... *hmmm, you probably made a deal with the Devil.* 12%

Arrrrg! Some angel's cell phone kept going off! 14%

May not add up to exactly 100% due to rounding and emotional distress from childhood Chick tract sessions.

A Joy of Tech Lexicon

After Y2K: The first webcomic by Nitrozac and Snaggy, which speculated what life would be like if the Millennium Bug had struck hard. The story follows a hapless geek and four beautiful and talented Techno-Talking Babes as they deal with the downfall of technology as we know it. Featuring many cameos from the Macintosh, Open Source, science, and science fiction communities.

All Your Base Station: Derived from the Internet saying "All Your Base are Belong to us." First appeared on a character's t-shirt in JoT #178.

AY2K: short form for the comic After Y2K.

Babe-dotted: The state of being swarmed by TTBs, as they flock to view your chick magnet (new hardware). Often an imaginary state, involving wishful thinking.

BFC: from Brute Force Compactor, JoT #340. SuperFlippy came up with the forum topic "Who would you want to BFC (Brute Force Compact)". Brilliant.

Blog Man: Someone who blogs continuously, so much so that they are highly likely to be unearthed in the year 2525, mummified in Blogger Position.

By The Beard Of Peter Gabriel!: Exclamation created by forum member GMx, after the appearance of our Peter Gabriel comic (JoT number #393) Later we made a little "smilie" for it for the Forums. That comic was enjoyed by bass player and music legend Tony Levin, who emailed us this: "Hi. I'm Tony Levin, bassist with Peter Gabriel. We're in rehearsals here in England, and just came across your site. I love the cartoon (not sure Peter will love it) that has his likeness... ....best wishes, keep up the good work. t.l. Cool!

Despicability Amplification Field: The antithesis of Steve Job's Reality Distortion Field. Currently generated by Bill Gates.

DNS Zone: The zone of nothingness that occurs when your DNS fails and your website becomes lost in the Internet ether.

Geekier than thou: Like the statement "holier than thou", superior in a geeky way.

Geeko Sapiens: The advanced form of homo sapian, one, which depends on its intellect and geeky prowess for survival.

Google Giggling: Using the search engine Google.com as a treasure hunt tool in order to find a joke or humorous image. For instance, instructing a friend to search Google using specific keywords or phrases, in an effort to guide them to a particularly funny result. Also known as Google-Gagging.

Great Wheels of Zeus! A homage to Clark Kent's boss Perry White's exclamation "Great Scott!", mixed in with a little Wozniakian reference.

The Ides of MacWorld: The period of time around MacWorld Expo in which the risk of Apple announcing a cancellation of hardware (such as the Cube) or software (such as iTools) is extremely high.

Jaguar Genius: The next generation of the Mac Genius, first suggested by Rednivek on the #joyoftech IRC channel, and immortalized by DigitalBill's comic appearance.

JoyBase: The insanely great online database of Joy of Tech comics created by Jonathon Bell, using PHP and MySQL. Can be accessed on the main JoT page, or via the Archives.

JoyChat: A simple to use IRC client for OS X, that connects one to the Joy of Tech chat channel on Slashnet, #joyoftech.

JoyPoll: The poll that appears with the web edition of the Joy of Tech, usually relating directly to the comic, and poking fun at the subject matter in a little more detail.

JoyPoll image: The randomly selected Joy of Tech graphic that appears in the JoyPoll. Occasionally, a comic is specifically created for that slot. Clicking on the graphic takes you back to the main Joy of Tech page.

JoyQuips: The humorous and sometimes sarcastic comments on the JoyPoll choices, only visible if you have done the JoyPoll.

JoyRounds: the reasons why the JoyPoll results "May not add up to exactly 100 percent." e.g. May not add up to exactly 100% due to rounding, and infectious Russian music.

JoT: short form of The Joy of Tech!

JoyWall: a mosaic of random Joythumbnails, which we sometimes post up if the online comic is delayed for some reason. Each time the page is reloaded, a new random mosaic of thumbnails is displayed, with each thumbnail linking to its appropriate comic. Uses a javascript created by SuperFan and great geek LostInColorado!

Mac Genius: Our variation of what was previously called the Apple Genius, someone who works at the Genius Bar in an Apple Store. For a brief period of time we sold the legendary Mac Genius t-shirt. Soon after, Apple registered Mac Genius as a service mark, serviced us a Cease and Desist, and began calling its geniuses Mac Geniuses. No, we aren't bitter.

Magnificent Valour!: First appeared on a Geek eCard, then became Snaggy's trademark congratulations. Its origins are from a Three Musketeer movie.

Nitrodotted: in the spirit of Slashdotting, having your webpage linked to by the main Joy of Tech comic, or from the AY2K comic page.

Nitrozac: Co-creator of the Joy of Tech and AY2K comics. Translation: A very powerful anti-depressant.

Nitrozac'd: Being drawn by Nitrozac, and featured in one of her comics. Has the effect of a very powerful anti-depressant.

Nitrozanium: The mysterious metal in the AY2K universe that surrounds Bill Gate's washroom. It is indestructible, and apparently of alien origin.

Panther Genius: The next generation of Mac prowess above Jaguar Genius. Yes, available in t-shirt form at the webstore.

Pre-Keynote Anxiety Disorder: A condition which many Mac geeks experience as they tremble, sweat, get light-headed, dizzy, and hyperventilate at the thought of what may or may not be announced at an Apple Expo.

Profanity Distortion Field: Those magical times when Steve Jobs flips like a switch and starts swearing like a truck driver.

Slippery with Drool: A sign first spotted in comic #104, signifying drool worthy hardware. Various adaptations have appeared since, usually in MacWorld Expo related comics.

Snaggy: Co-creator of the Joy of Tech and AY2K comics, derived from "Snagalena", which is a song Snaggy wrote. "The song is about a demented old cowboy who is singing a sad tale of a love gone away. His "love" just happens to be an alien who crash-landed into his cabin years earlier. The two of them had a variety of adventures together, although you're never quite sure if they were real, or perhaps the result of a series of experiments the alien performed on the

cowboy. My friend Meryn Cadell and I used to IRC... she started to call me Snaggy, and the nick stuck."

Snaggalite: A mysterious element from the cartoon universe that has yet to be fully explained. Not that anyone is in a hurry to do so.

Spammish: A language where you speak in titles derived from email spam JoT #264. ie: "Re: Our conversation yesterday, I'm sick of working for a living! Stay home and make great money!"

Spam-o-condriac: A phenomenon that occurs when the patient feels symptoms and anxiety described by the titles of spam emails he or she receives.

Spungo'd, Snupy'd or Cheezi'd: When a Forum thread gets hijacked, often in a twisted or perverted direction, and most often hilariously. Named after the masters of such hijacking, Forum members Spungo, Snupy, and cheezi git (btw, these forum members are brainy geeks, despite what you may read.)

SuperBlabberMouth: The title of a forum member who has reached a post count of 1000 or higher. Forum member Saintonge coined this phrase.

SuperFan: A wonderful, generous human being that voluntarily subscribes to JoT. Perks include a custom forum avatar and the secret password to the Super Fan Clubhouse (private forum). Our heroes!

Techno Talking Babe: An attractive woman who is also a techno wiz, or likes to talk about tech. Primarily describes Bambi, Brandi, Dawn, and Fawn, the immensely popular and attractive characters from AY2K, whose motto is "Smart = Sexy". Also describes most of the female members of our Forums.

Techno Talking Hunk: The hunk-of-burning-love type of man that is also a techno wiz and likes to talk about tech. Rare and elusive? Nope!

TTB: Short form of Techno Talking Babe.

TTH: Short form of Techno Talking Hunk.

Twin fantasy: Desiring a lusty encounter with a dual processor computer.